PSYCHIC SPY

The Story of an Astounding Man

PSYCHIC SPY

The Story
of an Astounding Man

CLIFFORD L. LINEDECKER

DOUBLEDAY & COMPANY, INC.
GARDEN CITY, NEW YORK 1976

ACKNOWLEDGMENTS

To Marty Gunther, my friend, who unselfishly gave of his time and skills to help in preparation of the manuscript.

To Kathy Morgan, who cheerfully, then doggedly, typed the manuscript.

To Monzel Wickliffe for being thoughtful of strangers.

Most of all, to Walter B. Gibson for opening necessary doors and making the book possible.

DESIGNED BY LAURENCE ALEXANDER

Library of Congress Cataloging in Publication Data
Linedecker, Clifford L
  Psychic spy.

  Bibliography
  1. Montgomery, Ernesto Alexander, 1925–
I. Title.
BF1283.M585L45   133.8′092′4
ISBN: 0-385-11457-5
Library of Congress Catalog Card Number 76-3003
Copyright © 1976 by Clifford L. Linedecker and
  Ernesto A. Montgomery

For Junko
My past, present and future.

Contents

Introduction

During more than two years as an articles editor for *The National Tattler*, specializing in parapsychology and the occult, I have come to know personally perhaps 100 psychics and healers.

I found some psychics to be personable but inaccurate and inept, usually believing in themselves, but with their psychic powers no more developed than those of the man or woman next door.

Others constantly amazed me with their ability to see into the future. They consistently charted the peccadillos of celebrities before they occurred, warned of disasters, worked with police to locate runaway, lost or murdered children and forecast political changes and the state of the economy with phenomenal accuracy. Often they prophesied events in my personal life.

Dr. Ernesto A. Montgomery, a clergyman and former member of the Jamaica Constabulary Force is one of these. He is one of the handful of psychics I learned to call on for a clairvoyant look into my personal life.

Some of his prophecies have been truly astonishing. Documented in daily and weekly newspapers, tabloids, magazines and on tapes of radio and television programs, a few of his more startling predictions included:

—The assassination attempt on Alabama Governor George Wallace.
—Admitting of Red China to the United Nations.
—Revolution in Chile.
—Deportation of Timothy Leary from Switzerland as an undesirable alien.
—The death of Aristotle Onassis.
—The second Arab–Israeli War.
—The death of Louis Armstrong.
—A prison riot resulting in the deaths of forty-three people. (Attica exploded in violence shortly after his prediction and forty-one guards and prisoners died, with the toll falling only two short of his prophecy.)
—Nomination of Senator George McGovern as Democratic presidential candidate, and the election of Richard M. Nixon in the 1972 elections.
—Election of a young Los Angeles city councilman as mayor (Tom Bradley).[1]

Often his worldwide predictions for print and electronic media are realized before they can be publicized. The October 12, 1975, edition of The National Insider related his August 26 prediction that deposed Emperor Haile Selassie I, of Ethiopia soon would die. Selassie, Conquering Lion of Judah, King of Kings, Elect of God, died in his sleep on August 27 at eighty-three.

There have been hundreds of others, including such world-shaking events as the assassinations of the Kennedy brothers and Martin Luther King and the Sharon Tate murders in Benedict Canyon.

Those, of course, are examples of prophecies involving individuals and events of great national or world interest. But there have been thousands of others that the Los Angeles prophet has made for men and women whose names never will be carried in newspaper headlines.

Secretaries, factory workers, bus drivers, housewives—all the so-called "little people," whose names are in the newspapers usually only when they are married or in obituaries when they die.

It is toward these people, too, that Dr. Montgomery concentrates his healing ministry.

Yet it was neither his healings nor his uncanny ability of prophecy that convinced me that he of all the psychics and healers I knew should be the subject of a book.

There are several who can match his record for accuracy and who also share certain of his other talents such as healing, psychometry and soul travel. What, then, was so special about Dr. Ernesto A. Montgomery? What was there in his background and experience that made him so different from the others?

Dr. Montgomery was a psychic spy for the British during World War II!

He was recruited into British Intelligence in the early 1940s, and spent his entire military career in Jamaica. As a skinny, knobby-kneed teen-ager, he used trance, deep meditation, psychometry and soul travel, projecting his etheric self out of body to spy on the enemy. His work and the work of those like him helped shorten World War II.

It sounded too incredible to believe. He dropped the information offhandedly during a telephone conversation. I had asked for some personal background to include in a story on end-of-the-year predictions I was compiling from various psychics.

He had first recounted his prediction in 1957 of a disastrous train crash in Jamaica, his fateful prophecies of the assassinations of the Kennedy brothers and his chilling augury of the Sharon Tate-LaBianca murders in California.

As an apparent afterthought, he then remarked: "Oh, yes. During World War II, I was a psychic spy for MI5, British Intelligence."

Frankly, I wasn't too impressed by the pronouncement. When talking to journalists and police, people sometimes remember things differently than they actually occurred. I didn't yet know Dr. Montgomery well enough to realize that his memory doesn't function that way.

It was not until later that I learned that if he doesn't remember something clearly, he says so. And more important, if his psychic powers aren't hitting on all six cylinders on a certain day or subject—and many psychics sometimes have bad days—he also says so. He doesn't bluff.

It was at least a couple of months before I happened to mention the conversation to Sybil Leek, the British-born astrologer and Witch now living in Florida. Sybil, too, had done some work for British Intelligence during World War II, I learned. What's more, she had worked with the late Ian Fleming, creator of the James Bond 007 series of spy novels. Dr. Montgomery had mentioned working with Fleming.

Belatedly, my interest was piqued. The conversation with Sybil Leek led to serious research. In hardly any time I had located others who had worked for British Intelligence as psychics or astrologers. Winston Churchill, I learned, was deeply interested in the occult. And the Nazis had an impressive network of occultists—some from as far away as Tibet—working for them during the war.

The book was on its way.

My first meeting with Dr. Montgomery was a surprise. I had known him previously only as a voice on the telephone with a formality and clipped accent that was impeccably British.

I found a nattily attired gentleman who always wore a suit with a fresh boutonniere and carried a rolled-up umbrella. I also found a warm human being.

He greeted everyone he met with an animated smile and friendly "hello," even people he passed in the parking garage of our hotel and on the street. He disregarded the suspicious frowns he received from some strangers in return.

"In Jamaica," he explained, "we always tip our hats to the ladies, and say 'hello' to everyone we meet."

He could be formal, especially when he was busy with his work. But I learned that he was also a person who could enjoy posing for pictures with his arm around the "Big Bad Wolf" during a visit to Disneyland. And he could switch quickly from serious talk of World War II, his ministry and his healings to his youth in Jamaica or to his favorite ride at the park—a trip through a West Indies pirates' lair in Fantasyland.

Whatever he does, prophecy, healing, preaching or fixing himself a Jamaican meal of fish and yams, he does it with enthusiasm. He absorbs himself in his project of the moment.

Dr. Montgomery, like most psychics, is better able to counsel and prophesy with consistent accuracy for strangers or people he does not know well, than he is for himself, family members or close personal friends. And being a psychic doesn't keep him from experiencing many of the little problems that hassle us ordinary mortals.

He can be absentminded. He can lose things. He has eaten burned rice and beans more than once after forgetting them on the stove while he was cooking. He has overslept, and he has been late for appointments.

While we were compiling the material for this book, he moved his offices from Los Angeles to Hollywood, and some important pictures and documentation were misplaced. He looked for them for two days before they were found. A psychic can begin second-guessing when working for himself.

Yet at other times he can receive sudden psychic warnings or insight into everyday matters that save him considerable difficulty. One evening as he was driving my wife and me along a Los Angeles highway to dinner at the home of friends in Toluca Lake, the arrow on his speedometer crept up over the fifty-five-mile-an-hour speed limit. He suddenly pressed the brakes, slowing the car abruptly. There was nothing immediately ahead of us, and I asked why he had slowed so suddenly.

"There is a police car waiting about a mile ahead of us," he said. "My antennae were hurting." A few minutes later, we passed the police car parked with its lights dimmed at the side of the highway.

Dr. Montgomery's antennae were another surprise that momentarily strained my credibility. They are flesh and bone appendages just above his ears. They throb when he is endangered in any way.

He hadn't mentioned the antennae before, and I hadn't noticed them. People find it hard to believe that they are real. I didn't believe either, until I gingerly lifted his hair just above his ears. There they were. I felt them with my fingers.

By this time, I was becoming desensitized to surprises and was ready to believe almost anything. So when he told me that he was a descendant of King Solomon and the Queen of Sheba, I didn't cast a single reproachful glance in his direction. I just listened. He explained that he is a reincarnation of the son of the biblical couple. Tracing his ancestry more conventionally through direct bloodlines, he added that he is the descendant of Negro slaves brought to the West Indies from the old Gold Coast, now Ghana.

Dr. Montgomery is an amazing, complex, engaging man. His experience as a psychic spy who eavesdropped on military secrets of the Axis powers with such esoteric and mystical techniques as trance, meditation and soul travel is hard to match for drama, mystery and excitement.

I hope you find reading his story to be as fascinating as I found it to be intriguing while putting it all together.

PART 1

The Boy Who Became a Psychic Spy

1

The Seer Who Saved D-Day

It was hot, the shimmering kind of heat that settles in near visible waves and distorts the vision. Eighteen-year-old Ernesto Montgomery was seated under a tree, back against the trunk, his knees upraised.

Clad in short light summer khakis, other members of the Drum and Bugle Corps of the Jamaican Home Guard also lounged lazily in the midday heat, sprawling in small clusters where they could find shade as they took a break following a long session of bugle practice.

Montgomery looked up as Lance Corporal Nunez, the corps' leading bugler, hurried to him from a tent several yards away.

"Godfather wants you," Nunez advised. "He say to hurry."

Minutes later Private Montgomery was standing at attention, his arms stretched stiffly at his sides along the sharp creases of his short khaki trousers, before "Godfather," his sergeant major.

Then he was hurrying down the hill toward the area where the white troops were billeted at garrison headquarters—and toward his most exhausting adventure as a psychic spy in World War II.

It was June 4, 1944, and Private Ernesto A. Montgomery, a fragile 116 pounds and five feet, eight inches tall, was not to see his fellow bugle corps members again for seven days. Not until almost a week after D-Day, June 6, 1944, the day two million soldiers from the United States, Britain, Canada, Free France and other Allied nations hit the beaches along a sixty-mile stretch of the Normandy coastline and became firmly established inland.

Casualties in the invasion were enormous on both sides. But they could have been much more devastating for the Allies if the assault had been postponed another day or longer. It might have been, if not for Private Montgomery and his psychic powers.

The time period allowable for the assault on mainland Europe was brief. Strategists headed by General of the Army Dwight D. Eisenhower agreed that the invasion, tabbed "Operation Overlord," had to be launched in May or early June if it was to give Allied troops time to gain a secure foothold and drive inland before winter.

The choppy English Channel was historically known for bad weather and sudden storms even in the summer months. The problem posed to the invaders was choosing a period of several days of relatively calm weather conditions. Otherwise, the assault would almost certainly end in terrible disaster for the Allies. May was the very soonest that tides and sunrise could be expected to offer optimum conditions for the assault.

By the time superiors called upon the young soldier-psychic for advice, a May invasion already had been scrapped, and hundreds of thousands of troops waited in England to board ships and landing craft poised for the choppy trip across the Channel.

After storms and other delays forced Eisenhower's command to scratch plans for a May invasion, June 5 was selected as a target date. But meteorological reports remained grim. Predictions that bad weather was on the way and was expected to continue through the first week of June left the Allied strategists deeply worried as the designated day for the invasion approached.

The Allies had gone to great trouble to convince the Germans that they planned to strike straight across the Channel toward the important French port of Calais instead of further south, where the invasion would actually occur. And Anglo-American military leaders still were hopeful that they could maintain some time element of surprise, despite the massed troops and supplies, which covered the South of England.

A postponement past June 7 could mean that the invasion would have to be put off for many months or abandoned entirely. Abandonment would mean that Allied troops would have to advance from Russia and through Italy in a much slower move on Germany. The war could be extended for months.

Every day of delay would also give the Germans more time to fortify their Normandy defenses and to direct their remaining aircraft against the massed invasion force.

When General Eisenhower met with his American and British commanders for the final conference early June 4 to determine the feasibility of launching the invasion the next morning as scheduled, the outlook was grim.

In *Crusade in Europe,* Eisenhower's history of World War II in Europe, the general recalled:

> Low clouds, high winds, and formidable wave action were predicted to make landing a most hazardous affair. The meteorologists said that air support would be impossible, naval gunfire would be inefficient, and even the handling of small boats would be rendered difficult. . . . Weighing all factors, I decided that the attack would have to be postponed.[1]

A few hours later, Private Ernesto Montgomery was reporting to a briefing room at garrison headquarters, where three somber men in civilian clothes greeted him. He already knew them as Lieutenant Colonel John Stephens, Major William Coxe, and Major Haig Wainwright.

The trio of officers motioned the private over to a large table map.

Carefully structured in three dimensions to illustrate the rough topography, the map showed a body of water and a rugged stretch of coastline. Little else. No names were there to designate beaches or to identify the area of the world it represented. Identification tags and pins had been removed.

There were a few brief words. The private ran his fingers

softly over the ridges and projections of the map, and—incredibly
—turned his back on the officers and walked away and into a
small officers' dayroom, shut the door and lay down on a couch.

He closed his eyes. In moments his breathing slowed, his
ebony skin took on an ashen look, and he lay as if dead.

He wasn't dead. But his soul had left his body to travel
other planes of existence in an undertaking that yogis, mystics
and other spiritual adepts have been performing for centuries.

In soul travel, Dr. Montgomery and others say, the soul is
able to leave the body for short periods and visit on any one of
several planes of existence.

On the astral plane and others, time and space do not exist.
One may see into the past and future as well as the present.

It was Montgomery's mission to travel on the astral plane to
determine what weather conditions would prevail over the English Channel on June 6 and to learn whatever other information
he could about the German defenses.

Less than a half hour after he had lain down, the young
Jamaican soldier walked back into the conference room and reported that the weather would be clear for thirty-six to forty-
eight hours on June 6 and 7 and that the Germans would be
taken by surprise.

On June 5, the day after Montgomery's astral spying mission, winds of near hurricane force hit the coastline on both sides
of the Channel, as predicted by meteorologists. Torrential rains
were whipped against the tons of piled supplies, making un-
paved roads a quagmire for trucks, tanks and marching soldiers
and bouncing great ships about on mountainous waves. An Allied invasion on June 5 would have been one of the greatest ca-
tastrophes of the war.

That day, General Eisenhower gave his commanders the go-
ahead to launch the greatest seaborne assault in the history of
the world only twenty-four hours later—June 6, 1944.

In his history of the war in Europe, Eisenhower wrote that
his staff of meteorologists advised him about the brief period of
relatively good weather between the June 5 storm and a new,
longer onslaught of bad weather. In his report, he made no mention of British Intelligence or of a teen-age Jamaican psychic.

Like Eisenhower, other military historians who recorded the war, pointedly left out the part played by psychics and astrologers in the Allied effort. Most of the information officially recording their role during World War II still reposes in classified files in Washington, D.C., and in London.

But Montgomery is well aware of the role he played in the decision to launch the invasion on June 6. "General Eisenhower's move to launch the attack when he did was a direct result of my work," says the psychic. "When I returned from the astral plane, I said: 'Yes. Launch the invasion. The weather will hold.'"

The young psychic cautioned that the invasion had to be launched without delay, not only because the weather would quickly turn bad again, but also because the Germans were on the verge of introducing frightening new weapons into the war against Britain.

In his soul travel, Montgomery observed the enemy's deadly new secret weapons in installations along the French coast, the V-1, a small pilotless airplane filled with high explosives, and the V-2 rocket. The first V-1, which had been used before, although against other countries, fell on London six days after the Normandy invasion. The first V-2, which fell at such high speed that there was no warning of the approach, hurtled toward the English homeland two months later. Both had a devastating effect on British morale, on the civilians under attack and on the men in uniform who were worried about the safety of their loved ones at home.

Montgomery's disclosures about the new weapons added confirmation to information gathered by more traditional intelligence methods. Imminent use of the new weapons was an important factor in the rush to invade.

Eisenhower later wrote that if the new weapons had been put into use six months earlier, the invasion of Europe would have been made more difficult, perhaps impossible.

Montgomery never worked as hard in his life as he did in the days preceding the invasion. He was constantly working, soul traveling on four different occasions, psychometrizing maps and going into deep trance several times.

Drawing on his psychic abilities to the utmost, he followed

the Allied soldiers through the crucial first week of the invasion and passed on reams of vital information about German troop movements, concentration, staff decisions, air and land strength. Other psychics elsewhere were doing similar work.

Superiors permitted Montgomery only to change clothes, grab a few moments of sleep and a bite to eat before deluging him with questions and sending him back to work on new problems.

So many soul projections in so short a time and the demand on his other psychic powers were a terrific drain on his energy. The silver cord attaching his soul to his physical body began to weaken. The only means of rebuilding psychic energy that the still young and unsophisticated sensitive knew was rest and meditation. Military Intelligence didn't give him time for that.

"I was so tired that I couldn't hold a rifle. I was walking into things. I would be in that condition when I would report and they would tell me that I had to astral project—or soul travel again," he says.

"My body has never been so wracked. I have never been so weak. I was completely exhausted when it was all over."

Although Montgomery may have been able to conserve and use his psychic energy more wisely if he had been more mature and experienced, his youth helped him quickly to rebuild his physical strength.

In a few days he was completely rested and was as energetic as ever. It was then, as the epochal Allied victory was reported and analyzed in newspapers and on radio, that the true importance of his contribution became apparent to him. He was proud of himself. He was nineteen years old and his performance had been an impressive one. He would have liked to brag a bit. But he couldn't talk to anyone about it. No one.

"It was frustrating, as a young kid knowing that I was playing such a dramatic part in the war, and I couldn't even tell anyone," he remembers. "But we were sworn to secrecy."

The work of psychics and astrologers with British Intelligence was one of the most closely guarded secrets of World War II. Today, thirty years after the end of the conflict, their work is still clouded in mystery.

Montgomery was the only psychic working with five astrologers in a unit of Britain's Military Intelligence, MI5, in Jamaica. Each man functioned independently, and one was never told of the advice or predictions of the others.

There were brief introductions, bypassing names, when Montgomery came into the unit. After that, members seldom saw each other. On the few occasions when they did meet, they used code names.

"Everyone was very tight-lipped. I could not ask a question about anything for which I didn't need to know the answers," Dr. Montgomery says. "They had what they called a 'need to know' rule, and they only told you what was absolutely necessary. We were there to answer questions, not to ask them."

Montgomery was told enough so that he realized that other psychics and astrologers were working for MI5 around the globe. Most are still reluctant to talk about their experiences, although at least three others now living in the United States have disclosed some information about their work with British Intelligence during the war.

Count John Manolesco is one of those who has been willing to talk.

Now living in California, he was a young university student at the London School of Economics training to be an accountant and statistician, when he was approached by the Rumanian ambassador. The ambassador asked if he would agree to be trained as an astrologer and work with the British War Office. (Rumania later joined the Axis powers, and the ambassador was withdrawn from England.)

Manolesco was Rumanian-born but held British citizenship and was an announcer with the British Broadcasting Corporation in addition to his studies. He agreed to take a crash course in statistical astrology with a half-dozen other young economics students and to co-operate with the War Office.

"This was a very useful method of astrology devised by Karl N. Krafft, a Swiss genius recruited by the Nazis early in the war," recalls Manolesco. "He would come up with statistical probabilities based on the position of the planets and horoscopes, and the information was influential not only in strategical matters but also in Hitler's choice of generals and the interaction in the Führer's cabinet.

"One of our big hits was Hitler's choice of General Erwin Rommel to head the African campaign. And we also forecast the invasion of Crete. It could have been saved, but the Navy was not that much of a believer in astrology and did not take the necessary action to save it."

Count Manolesco recalls that Krafft was recruited by Rudolf Hess, once Deputy Führer of the Third Reich. Later, Krafft worked closely with Joseph Goebbels, the Nazi propaganda minister, and Heinrich Himmler, head of the SS and of the Nazi Occult Bureau.

Krafft forecast the assassination attempt on Hitler's life in early 1939, which the Nazi leader escaped by leaving a celebration in the Munich Beer Cellar minutes before a bomb exploded. From that time on, the Swiss astrologer exerted an extremely strong influence over the Führer.

"The British did not believe in astrology at that time but they wanted us to tell them what Hitler would be advised by his astrologers," Manolesco says.

Hungarian-born Louis de Wohl was one of the astrologers who worked for the British, casting horoscopes in an attempt to anticipate advice being passed on to Hitler. But De Wohl and other Allied astrologers also originated work of their own.

De Wohl claimed that although his primary mission was to counter the work of Hitler's astrological advisers, he provided other information, such as foretelling the result of the battle of Alamein. The information, he said, was obtained by comparing the horoscopes of Britain's General Sir Bernard L. Montgomery and General Rommel.

Sybil Leek, Witch, psychic and astrologer, also found herself using her occult arts on behalf of British Intelligence during the war. But more of that later.

One of those who still talks only guardedly about her World War II experiences with British Intelligence, is a part-time instructor at an American university better known for her research and skill as a lecturer and writer than for her abilities as a psychic. She has a Ph.D. from a foreign university.

Although her name is known to the author, her request for anonymity will be respected here. She prefers to keep her psychism secret from all but her family and close associates.

Dr. Shafica Karagulla, a close friend, tells of her experience with British Intelligence in *Breakthrough to Creativity: Your Higher Sense Perception.*

The friend, whom Dr. Karagulla describes with the pseudonym "Vicky," worked in England with a highly placed member of MI5 and another man who held an important job with the War Office.

Both men were psychics, as was she. According to Dr. Karagulla, the trio would meet, select their problem, and then use their individual methods of psychically looking for answers. Their findings would be written on separate pieces of paper, which would then be placed face down on a table. When each had concluded his or her work, the papers would be compared and discussed.[2]

In a brief interview for this book, the parapsychologist and psychic confirmed she was the "Vicky" of Dr. Karagulla's book but hesitated to disclose more information about her work with British Intelligence.

"It was other people connected with the government who made the decisions. Most of the time, the people with special abilities just gave advice," she explained.

"A lot of people have these ESP abilities and just keep quiet about it, but do their job. Other people around them conclude they know their business. But the professional person is not going to say she has ESP," she said, explaining her reticence to disclose her identity. "It could discredit her in her work."

She said she did not work as a member of a formal psychic unit for British Intelligence. "The people who did these things didn't call themselves 'psychics.' What happens is that the people who have these abilities are usually people who just appear especially capable in their jobs. This is why the government would deny it had a psychic unit," she said. "People working right beside them would deny they were doing anything special."

Montgomery, Manolesco and De Wohl's associates, of course, knew exactly what they were doing. But the knowledge was screened from all but a handful of key people. And according to Manolesco, each member of the "Psychological Unit," to which he was attached, who knew about the use of astrology in the war against the Axis, was required to sign a document agreeing to a twenty-year oath of secrecy.

Montgomery signed a document pledging him to secrecy for twenty years or longer, but today he sees no need to continue the silence. The Soviets, Americans and other world governments are now using psychic spys or are experimenting with the concept, and he believes that the work of Allied psychics and astrologers thirty years ago should become a recognized component of the history of World War ii.

2

The Boy with Psychic Eyes

ERNESTO ALEXANDER MONTGOMERY WAS BORN OCTOBER 2, 1925, in the tranquil village of Spalding, eighty-five miles west of Kingston, the capital of Jamaica. It was a land of sharp contrasts.

Rich, fertile topsoil supported luxurious rain forests, resplendent with orchids, dozens of varieties of spectacular flowering trees, mangoes and plantains. All were played against jagged dinosaur peaks and savannahs that rolled toward shoreline cliffs and wide, white beaches.

Jamaica was discovered by Columbus in 1494, but became a British possession after capture in 1655. The Arawak Indians who inhabited the island in the fifteenth century died or were killed after arrival of the Europeans. They were replaced by black Africans.

Three centuries of slave trade had uprooted thousands of Africans and brought them to the New World to cultivate sugarcane, coffee, bananas and spices for the "bushas," or white plantation owners.

Although freed with the abolition of slavery in 1833, black Jamaicans were still little more than chattel for their white employers. Blacks accounted for more than three quarters of the population, but had no say in the crown colony, which had been governed by martial law since Negro uprisings that coincided with the American Civil War. East Indians and Chinese, who also had come reluctantly in indentured servitude a decade before, a smattering of Lebanese and Jews, and of course the English Government officials and landowners, filled out the remainder of the population.

Like the Indians before them, black Jamaicans were skilled in using local plant life for home remedies to deal with almost any ailment.

If a child became ill with fever, his mother or father would walk into the brush to pick the long-bladed fever grass. The leaves would be boiled in clear water, which they carried in kerosene cans from crystalline rivers and wells. The child would then be set on a scrub board placed across the tub, where he would be enveloped in steam from the piping-hot brew and covered with a sheet or blanket until the water cooled. Twenty-four hours after the steamy treatment, the fever would be gone.

Women gathered cherita bark and made a punch for intestinal ailments. Everyone knew the secrets of the herbs. Everyone could pick them.

Jamaicans kept mistletoe in their homes. If a young girl was courting and was in a hurry to get her boyfriend to marry her, it was said that she had only to maneuver him under the mistletoe. The wedding was sure to follow soon.

The "Busha," "Mas' Charlie," lived like royalty as he extracted every bit of strength he could from his dark-skinned workers in the fields. In return he provided more conventional, improved medical care, mint teas and the mongoose. The mongoose was imported to fight snakes, which were taking a heavy toll of valuable slaves.

The busha introduced parliamentary procedure and open forums, which flourished in Kingston's Queen Victoria Park, where anyone who desired could climb onto a podium and speak. He imported the English language, which was quickly blended with African words to form a colorful local patois.

But 1925 was still several years before the political arrival of Alexander Bustamante, the Caucasian Jamaican of Portuguese-

German descent who became the island nation's first prime minister and was eventually knighted by the British queen. It was Bustamante whose alarm at the starvation wages black Jamaicans received for their back-breaking labor in the fields, the sugar refineries and the docks—about thirty-six cents a week —who organized the working classes.

Ernesto Montgomery was still an adolescent when Bustamante began his struggle for adult suffrage, Jamaican home rule and, finally, independence.

Ernesto's father, Isaac Montgomery, worked in the fields of the "busha." He died before his only son was five. The elder Montgomery was fortunate enough to own a small plot of land, on which he grew bananas, sugarcane, ackee, breadfruit and susumba, a plant that produces a small bulblike fruit, which Jamaicans cook with codfish and consider a great delicacy. He would work this land after a day under the blistering sun in Mas' Charlie's fields for thirty-six cents a week.

Emily Smith Montgomery went to the United Fruit Company fields at sunup with her husband. She would hoe while he forked. On their own small farm, she worked, too, preparing calalu, a Jamaican spinach. Isaac refined his sugar. He taught Emily how to boil cane. Together they poured the residue off the top of the concoction to make molasses and from the molasses, rum.

They fished in fresh-water ponds, ate afoo, a yam that grows from six inches to one foot long. Emily Montgomery boiled white yams until they dissolved into an excellent soup, or cooked succulent negro-yams. She made sweet-sap and sour-sap juices, both great delicacies, prepared black, bombay, kidney and many other varieties of mangoes, which grew wild.

A deeply religious woman, Mrs. Montgomery often worked until sunset, only to return home, prepare the family meal and then walk to a worship service miles away. Sometimes she rode astride a donkey or on horseback. The child, Ernesto, sometimes tagged along. Jamaicans did not often depend on conventional roads. They preferred to take shortcuts marked by piles of stones through the bush.

From the moment Ernesto Montgomery was born, the men

and women of Spalding, Manchester Parish, knew that he possessed special powers given to him by God. He was born with "the veil," a membrane that covered his face and is considered in most societies to be an indication of supernatural abilities. The membrane was easily disposed of. But the memory and expectations lingered.

What the baby's parents and friends didn't know was that at some time in his early childhood he would also inexplicably develop two small antennae.

Even Dr. Montgomery himself doesn't know when the strange inch-and-a-half-long appendages developed, but he remembers that they first became a factor in his life as a clairvoyant when he was about six. "The older I got, the more sensitive they became. Sensitive to touch, as well as psychically."

The boy learned that he could press his fingers to the gristlelike protuberances and pick up psychic vibrations of future events.

He learned to foretell the outcome of cricket matches when the North Street Congregational School played other schools. Not only that, but he knew in advance just how many wickets a bowler would get in a game.

On Fridays, when the weekly bicycle races were staged, his friends sometimes would borrow a shilling or so from their mothers' sugar bowls and gamble on the outcome. Betting only on the cyclists recommended by Ernesto, they never lost. As soon as the race was over and the bet paid, they would run home, replace their mothers' money and have enough left over to buy ice cream for everyone.

Although his friends all were aware that he was "smart," and somehow knew things in advance, he learned early not to talk about his antennae or to point them out to other children. The few times that he did show them to playmates, they teased or tried to pull them.

His mother was hardly aware of the sensitive area behind his ears. Emily Montgomery, with two daughters, Daisy and Violet, in addition to her son, was busy day and night working in the fields and caring for her home and family. She died shortly before Ernesto's eleventh birthday.

Despite the illiteracy of his parents, Ernesto had proved his brilliance before he was three by learning to read and write. This convinced his parents of one thing: he must attend school. He must have an education, even though this was a luxury unavailable to many Jamaican children fifty years ago.

Young Ernesto wasn't always that appreciative of his special status as a student. Unsurprisingly, there were mornings when he found it more appealing to sleep late, rather than to rouse himself out of bed and trudge off to a dreary classroom. On those mornings, after repeated warnings and with the time rapidly approaching when she had to leave for the fields, Emily Montgomery would drag her son out of bed, stand him on the floor and with one hand holding him solidly by an ear, dress him with the other hand.

In primer school he rapidly developed a compulsion to learn. He became a good student, although sometimes a disruptive one. Unfortunately for the decorum of the class, he often blurted out the answers to questions before his teacher could finish asking them.

By the time he was five, Ernesto could recall names of places and people he had heard only once. Before long he was astounding older residents of Spalding with his uncanny ability to predict exactly when hurricanes or other severe storms would strike the village. If a neighbor was about to die, by illness or accident, the boy would speak innocently of their "going away" soon.

When the devastating hurricane of 1933 struck other areas of the West Indies, Ernesto warned that Jamaica would not escape the destruction. The storm, he said, would veer and smash into the island, causing heavy property damage and loss of life. The word was quickly spread. The storm veered, as he said it would, and hit the island with its full fury. It was one of the most destructive hurricanes in the history of Jamaica.

People began to seek out the boy. They would be waiting for him when he got out of school. Strangers would follow him home, asking about errant husbands, lazy wives, lovers, money, illness. At night there would be tapping at the window, and a man or woman would be there when the child's mother looked out. "Miss Emily?" they would say. "I want to talk to your boy."

It was all fun for him. He would tell anyone anything they wanted to know for a smile or a lollipop.

It was quite another thing to his mother. Her son's studies were being interrupted, she was being bothered at work and the entire family was losing sleep. The family, now minus the husband and father, moved to Christiana, another village fifteen miles away.

Ernesto easily made friends in Christiana. After an evening meal of peas and rice, he and his friends would play. As often as not, they would watch one of the village magicians perform.

One time a young man still in his apprenticeship entertained the villagers with a rope trick. The stunt called for the rope to be looped and tied around his neck, then pulled taut by six men, three on each side, so that it appeared that he would be strangled. The secret was a special knot which would slip at the last moment.

The men jerked at the rope, almost hoisting the magician off his feet. He gagged. The men put more muscle into it, hunching their shoulders with the strain. The sweat glistened on their backs. The young man's eyes bulged. His face turned ashen. The spectators convulsed with laughter. It looked so real. The magician's tongue slipped from his mouth. There was a hoarse croak. The laughter died. So did the magician.

Ernesto's time in Christiana was brief. At religious meetings, he had learned somehow to use his hidden powers to heal the sick. The boy had only a hazy understanding of what he was doing. He knew that when he placed his hands on a sick man or woman and concentrated that they usually got better. He was told that God used him as a channel to heal. But he didn't know that healing was robbing him of his energy and draining his strength.

Emily Montgomery was concerned about his puny condition, but she did not realize that his poor health was involved with his healing work. And other problems were also beginning to develop.

In school, Ernesto began to use his psychic abilities again to beat classmates to the answers of questions. He told his friends about things that were going to happen in the future. He told them about surprise tests, and forecast their marks. Crowds began to gather around the family's little house again.

This time Emily put her son on a bus and sent him to Kingston, a hundred miles east, along the ocean. She had arranged for him to stay with her sister and brother-in-law.

Ernesto's aunt Ethel, like his mother, was a religious woman, deeply involved in the activities of various Christian sects that flourished on the island. Sometimes she attended meetings with her husband, James Cohen, but more often she went alone or with friends. Ernesto's uncle James was a dedicated lodge man. He was even more seriously dedicated to the rum bottle. The lodge and the bottle, Ernesto observed, did not leave much time for his wife's religious gatherings.

Fraternal organizations are an important part of the Jamaican culture. Another British import, they are respected as character builders, and are valuable in the teaching of parliamentary procedure.

Deprived of an older man's guidance since his father's death, Ernesto was delighted with his uncle, and intrigued by his involvement with fraternities. He quickly joined the juvenile branch of the Supreme Benefit Association, to which his uncle belonged. He became its youngest president.

James Cohen accepted the addition to his family with an easy tolerance and only an occasional outburst of pique at Ernesto's childish peccadillos.

One day the boy was playing when his uncle called for a glass of water. Ernesto was preoccupied climbing a guincâ tree for its sweet fruit. When he finally got around to the glass of water, his uncle was angry and boxed him on the ears.

Ernesto dropped to the floor, his feelings hurt as badly as his boxed ears and antennae, and feigned unconsciousness. His alarmed aunt and uncle rushed him to Dr. J. P. Walsh on Duke Street. The doctor discovered the boy's antennae.

Puzzled, he examined them, decided they were unnecessary and advised that they could be removed by a simple operation. Ernesto panicked and started to scream. When he was finally calmed, his guardians and the doctor agreed to let the antennae remain as long as they did not adversely affect his health. It was then that Ernesto first heard them referred to as antennae, by Dr. Walsh.

In Kingston, the more urbane city dwellers at first paid little attention to the amazing powers of prophecy demonstrated by young Ernesto. He made friends and often swam naked with them under a favorite culvert at the foot of Gold Street. The water and power department had installed the culvert to cool its equipment, and the water was always warm.

He attended North Street Congregational School, but drew little attention to himself although he was predicting sweeping changes in the British-controlled Jamaican Government.

No one took him too seriously because it would be years before his clairvoyance was proven correct.

Roman Catholicism and many traditional Protestant denominations abound on the island. But many West Indians preferred worshiping God as members of smaller, more unique sects.

Singing, dancing, hand clapping and testimonials all played an important part in the religion of Jamaica. Salvation Army bands competed on street corners with Pocomanians and Rastafarians and conventional Christians of dozens of different persuasions. The Rastafarians were generally looked down upon by other Jamaicans, the boy observed, and regularly clashed with the law.

The Rastafarians sincerely believed that Haile Selassie, the late monarch of Ethiopia, was God. They based their belief on the fact that he was then the only living black ruler whose life could be linked directly with the biblical King and Queen of Sheba. The Jamaican Rastafarians accepted literally as fact that he was King of Kings, Lion of Judah and could do no wrong.

One group of Rastafarians smoked "ganja," the highly potent Jamaican marijuana, using it much as the Indians of the American Southwest and Mexico use peyote, mushrooms and jimsonweed to experience psychedelic religious ecstasy. Unfortunately for the "Rastas" they also experienced frequent police raids.

Nevertheless the unique Rastafarian theology appealed to
many Jamaicans who were convinced that Africa was heaven
and who wanted to return there to the Promised Land. No African nation would accept them, however, since most African nations were experiencing domestic instability.

In Kingston and in the villages, even the "Pocos" and the
"Rastas" stood aside for white-robed men and women who
would sometimes appear in the streets wailing Cassandra-like of
misfortune to come: of drought, of storms, of disease, of personal
tragedies. These were "warners," mortals who received spiritual
messages directly from God. Their wailing cries could be heard
blocks away, and they were never ignored.

Introduced early to the religions of the island by his mother
and his aunt, Ernesto developed a perceptive spirituality and tol-
erant philosophy recognizing that there are many paths to the
Godhead.

He also learned to play the drum, the most common instru-
ment for making the music that inevitably accompanied the religious meetings.

Before his ninth birthday, he joined Mother Ida's Spiritual
Mission, a non-denominational Christian group, with headquarters at 43 Pink Lane in Kingston. Mother Ida had followers
in towns and villages throughout the island.

It was easy to join. Raising her voice over the rhythmic beat
of the drums, Mother Ida would call for converts. In response,
those about to be saved would rise from their chairs, walk to the
front of the hall and kneel before the drum. All those souls who
accepted Christ immediately became "believers." Baptism was
next, and the dripping neophyte or believer would emerge from
the water as one of Mother Ida's Saints.

Clad in white from head to foot, Mother Ida and her Saints
held frequent pilgrimages to locations considered to be especially holy, and often abstained from eating for long periods of
time during religious fasting.

Once every three months, Mother Ida would lead a pilgrim-
age to the Hope River, about nine miles from Kingston, to a location near where the University of the West Indies is today. It

was there that Mother Ida, standing on the bank as her Saints waded into the clear water, would call believers to baptism.

When Ernesto Montgomery was dunked beneath the surface to receive the Holy Ghost, he was nine years old. Although he remained frail and sickly, the baptism had a profound effect on his spiritual being. Immediately his psychic powers and intellect improved. He left the water in a trance, speaking in tongues, a completely different person. From that point on he became even more aware of the spiritual world around him and answered the questions of those who came to him for advice with more maturity and insight.

Ernesto enjoyed being a drummer for Mother Ida. He beat the bass as she and elder Saints led baptisms. He watched, wide-eyed, as others were stricken with the Holy Ghost. He saw men and women dipped below the water as sinners and saw them emerge filled with the mysterious powers of the Holy Ghost, speaking foreign tongues that sounded as strange to him as Chinese or Japanese.

It was during Mother Ida's missions that his healing powers first began to manifest themselves, although he did not realize it until he was much older. Jamaicans came from all over to be cured. He saw people approach Mother Ida's healers, bent over in pain. They left screaming praise for Jesus and leaping in ecstasy. Others hobbled up to the healers on crutches and after a few uncertain steps walked away without them.

After Mother Ida died, Ernesto continued to play drums for Sister Joyce and a "brother," who served as her joint spiritual successors. No one in the congregation, including the leaders, had received formal religious training. It was enough to gather and worship the Almighty as best they knew.

By the time Ernesto was eleven, with his mother gone and now permanently in the care of his aunt, he was playing hooky from school to go to Queen Victoria Park.

Laid out along East Queen Street in downtown Kingston, the park was cool and inviting, with impeccably manicured lawns in the British custom and dozens of brightly painted benches where people could sit and take their leisure.

But the primary appeal was the speakers. Every day was

soapbox forum day in Queen Victoria Park. Amateur or professional orators could climb onto a soapbox or bench or just find a spot of high ground and deliver a harangue about anything from the ills of British Colonial rule, immigration and Communism to polygamy or runaway wives.

No one was promised a crowd, but each of the dozens of forums occurring simultaneously usually attracted at least a half-dozen or so onlookers, who would sometimes clap and yell in approval—and sometimes jeer.

No one jeered or clapped for "Nine Day," when he held court in the park. Nine Day was an obeah man, the meanest, most menacing practitioner of Jamaican Voodoo on the island. There were few men or women on Jamaica who hadn't heard of him, and almost none of those who weren't afraid of him. Fear was one of his most effective weapons.

A huge, barrel-shaped man about thirty-five years old, Nine Day was said to be a cold-blooded killer. Killing was all he ever did.

Other obeah men and women did love or lust spells. They would break up marriages, bind weakened marriages, hex quarrelsome neighbors, seduce virgins, heal illnesses, curse a cruel employer, fashion a good luck talisman or amulet for a client. But Nine Day was a specialist. He did only one thing, it was said, and he did it well. He killed.

If two men would get in a swearing match, and one of them, in anger, would call out, "Nine days," the quarrel would end abruptly. The man who had been threatened would blanch, turn and begin clearing up his personal affairs. He knew that as soon as his enemy passed a few shillings to Nine Day, that only nine days later he would be leaving this world.

When Nine Day called out a man's name in the park, it was the call of death. The victim's family would wail and begin saying tearful good-bys. It would do no good even if a wife, parent, son or daughter were brave enough to plead with Nine Day. Neighbors and friends would avoid the victim. They treated him as if he were already dead.

In nine days the victim would die. There would be no gradual wasting away, no apparent illness. He might just lie down in his bed on the ninth day, or be walking on the street—and die. Nine Day never failed.

His reputation for evil was so strong that no other obeah men or women dared to oppose him. None of them would do protective or uncrossing spells for his would-be victims. No one wanted to be his enemy.

Policemen, like everyone else, dealt respectfully with Nine Day, although they arrested him often. Obeah was against the law, and practitioners were subject to flogging and imprisonment. Nine Day didn't seem to mind. He had a law all his own.

Ernesto Montgomery stayed out of his way. It took the boy years to realize that the only protection he needed was the power he received from God.

"Elephant" was another, less threatening character who inhabited the park. He weighed more than four hundred pounds, was an imbecile and sat in the park night and day with a little bag slung over his shoulder. People would give him food, which he put in the bag or ate immediately.

Miss Woodbine outweighed Elephant by two hundred pounds, but she never came to the park. She couldn't. She was so big that she couldn't get out of her house on Spanish Town Road. Ernesto was about seven years old when she died, and men had to knock the side of her house down to get her out. She was so enormous, they had to rig a block and tackle.

Reggie, the short-legged man, passed by Elephant and other denizens of the park several times every day. He walked purposefully, with quick short steps. He could cover a mile in little more than five minutes without running. His specialty was picking up cigarette butts. Whenever he spotted one, he picked it up quick, scooping it into his hand, without breaking stride.

Even Reggie stopped to watch when Dr. Splume was performing. Dr. Splume was a favorite with the children. Whenever Dr. Splume was about, he would be surrounded by a crowd of youngsters.

Unconcerned with the ninety-degree temperatures, Dr. Splume always wore a long leather coat, let his hair grow long, and sang and leaped. He was a street side entertainer who lived off the coins people threw at his feet.

He would pick a busy location in the park or climb on the steps of someone's front porch and start talking. His speech was fast and rhythmic, and as the crowd gathered, the talk would become song. He would announce that he was going into the "bim."

As the onlookers tossed pennies, shillings and sixpence pieces at him he would sing:

> Roll Jordan, Roll.
> Roll Jordan, Roll
> If you want to go to
> Heaven when you die,
> To hear when Jordan roll.

Bim.

As he shouted "bim," he would leap three or four feet, straight up, arms pressed against his lanky sides. The more money that was tossed at him, the louder the "bims," and the higher he leaped. When the money was flying and the "bim" was working well, Dr. Splume would launch himself six feet or more straight up. He would come down in slow motion.

At Dr. Splume's urging, the crowd would take up the "bim." Dr. Splume would shout "bim" and leap into the air. The crowd would echo "bim" and toss coins. As Dr. Splume's bony body would settle back to the porch or sidewalk and his knees would buckle to begin another spring, his long arms would reach out and pluck up the coins without breaking his rhythm.

"Bim!" he would shout, leaping. "Look at bidda, badda bo. Bim! Artitiie me, bidda badda bo. Bim!"

Unfortunately, Dr. Splume was shot to death one day by a policeman.

In 1935 Ernesto was ten years old and already knew that a world war was approaching. Hitler had just sent his troops into the Rhineland when the youngster's clairvoyant powers told him that Britain and the U.S. would soon be involved in one of the most destructive wars in the history of mankind.

The boy confided in G. D. Dawkins, the principal of North Street Congregational School. Many lives would be lost, the child advised soberly, but the British and their Allies would eventually triumph.

Four years later, as he had predicted, Britain and almost all of Europe were in the war. Oratory at Queen Victoria Park became even more spirited, the crowds larger.

By this time one of the most intriguing orators was fourteen-year-old Ernesto Montgomery. A child among grown men. Daily, the adults discussed, analyzed and debated the war news read in the newspapers the night before. The boy orator discussed the war dispatches in tomorrow's newspaper. Somehow, visions of battles not yet fought filled his mind.

As the youngster's predictions began to be borne out by events more people came to the park to listen. They began to call him "the genius." It certainly seemed that he was. Even though he had no knowledge of the rudiments of warfare, he predicted with uncanny accuracy the movements of individual divisions and pinpointed concentrations of enemy troops. He knew in advance which country would be attacked next by the Germans. He knew what the outcome would be.

For two years, older men listened with increasing respect. They did not fully comprehend how their "genius" was able to foresee the future. It was enough to listen and to watch. They knew that he was seldom wrong.

The one thing the boy could not foresee was his own impending involvement in the conflict and the significant role he was to play in its conclusion.

Shortly after his sixteenth birthday, he was to disappear from Queen Victoria Park. He was to become a special soldier. He awaited a special fate.

3

Jamaica: A Psychic Spy

THE DAY WASN'T AN UNTYPICAL ONE. THE FRAIL, STRING bean-thin youth wandered home to 25 Rose Lane from Queen Victoria Park, his thoughts more on the waiting supper of peas and rice neighbors had been preparing for him since his aunt Ethel died than on the day spent debating older men about the war in Europe.

Even the thoughts of peas and rice fled when he saw the letter.

Young Ernesto Montgomery had received letters before, many of them, from people with personal problems they hoped he would solve: troubles with husbands or wives, questions about the future, or illnesses. Those who included return postage with their queries received replies. But this letter was different. There were no questions. Instead, there was an order. An order to report to the training center of the Jamaica Home Guard for a pre-induction physical examination the next day.

The neighbors were upset and worried. The boy was under-age. Barely sixteen. And undersize. He was so fragile, thin and sickly-looking at 110 pounds that if the enemy ever captured him, the neighbors teased, they would throw him back for sure.

They couldn't conceive of the Home Guard being interested in the skinny boy, much less actually inducting him. They were certain that after the officers took one look at his bony frame they wouldn't even complete the examination. The neighbors were wrong.

One week later he became Private Ernesto A. Montgomery. But in so doing he proved his neighbors partially right. One look at the skinny runt reporting for his physical and the captain in charge admitted he couldn't imagine why the Home Guard wanted him. A higher ranking officer called the captain over. Two more officers joined them.

The captain's attitude suddenly changed. Montgomery was good army material after all, it seemed. He directed the skinny youth to a desk and handed him a sheaf of papers, a pencil, and told him to fill out a written test. A few hours later Montgomery was stepping off a bus at the Upper Park Camp, where other black soldiers in the Home Guard were quartered.

There he was separated from other potential inductees and given a medical examination by a Captain Rose. "He was a very nice man. Very courteous," Montgomery remembers. Everyone there was nice and courteous that day.

The test completed, Montgomery was told to return home and that he would hear from the induction center soon.

A few days later he was sworn into the Home Guard.

Despite his small size, the new private moved easily through the ensuing weeks of basic training. He was kept too busy with obstacle courses, rifle training, marching drill and instruction as a coast watcher tracking shipping off the coast of the island colony, to wonder much about why he was inducted or about the special attention he had received.

After primary training he was assigned to the Drum and Bugle Corps. Montgomery already played the drum, and had since he was a small boy with Mother Ida's Saints.

When he was six or seven years old he and other children fashioned their own drums from small pans or by cutting condensed milk cans in half, stretching a cloth over the openings and holding it down with clay. While adults played drums of wood or metal with goatskin heads, the children used their more primitive instruments during the testimony of Saints or new converts.

When he was older he used a pan which previously had been filled with grain for pigeons and was set on the front veranda of his house. It became a side drum. "I play that one with my foot and the other drum with my hands. And when people passed it was beautiful," Montgomery remembers. "But in the Guard I had to learn a different way."

There was little about his experience in the Home Guard that went as he had expected it. Ernesto didn't share his neighbors' reservations about his induction. Instead, he eagerly anticipated the experience and looked forward to the glamour and excitement of military life.

At the time, many Jamaicans not much older than he were being sent to England to serve in the Royal Air Force. This was the type of adventure meant for him, Ernesto told himself.

But he was not to leave Jamaica until long after the war was over, long after he was discharged from the Home Guard.

He applied for the RAF. Periodically orders would be posted on company bulletin boards, and the recruits would search the lists for their names. Whoops of excitement broke from the mouths of the young soldiers who found their names on the list of those orders to England and the RAF or for other assignments promising adventure away from the island. But Private Montgomery's name never was among them.

Attached temporarily to the band, he waited and wondered, trying to figure out why he consistently was passed over. It was ten weeks after his induction before he learned why he had been drafted.

Perched on the edge of his bunk, he was rubbing brass polish onto the already shiny surface of his newly issued bugle during the few minutes left before lunch. The giant form of Sergeant Major Rowe loomed in the entranceway of the tent.

A broad-shouldered, light-skinned career soldier, Rowe always seemed to be smiling. Although a professional in every sense, Rowe did not fit the usual picture of the sadistic topkick who took pleasure in making life miserable for his subordinates. Instead, his huge presence hovered over the youthful recruits like a giant mother hen. He was more likely to get them out of trouble than he was to create problems by overstressing discipline or military order. In private, the neophyte guardsmen referred to him as "Godfather."

This time, however, his usually cheerful face was creased with worry. Sweat rolled down his broad cheeks. The message was so urgent that instead of sending an orderly, the sergeant major himself had hurried across the parade ground in the blistering sun to deliver it.

Montgomery was summoned to the base commander's office immediately. And when a raw recruit was summoned before Captain Scudamore, it usually meant trouble. Trouble so big that even Godfather couldn't resolve it.

Shakily, Private Montgomery reported to the base commander's office. Scudamore ordered him to change quickly to civilian clothes and hurry to garrison headquarters.

White troops exclusively operated garrison headquarters. Units such as the Welsh Guard, the King's Shropshire Light Infantry, Canadians, New Zealanders and other British Commonwealth brigades served six-month tours as they manned the station, which served as operations center for the entire Caribbean area. Black Jamaican soldiers were a rarity on garrison grounds, especially sixteen-year-old recruits.

Private Montgomery was sure he knew the reason he was called to garrison. Obviously he finally had been selected for England and the RAF. Admittedly the civilian clothes puzzled him, but he was certain there was a good reason. There was!

His bewilderment increased after a guard escorted him into the headquarters building. When the recruit snapped to attention to greet a British Army major, the officer responded by stepping forward and shaking his hand.

"Now, this was something new to me," Montgomery recalls. "In the Army, especially the British Army, you don't fraternize. When you greet a British officer and he speaks to you, you stand at attention until he is through talking.

"When I saw him I snapped to attention fast—and at that psychological moment he grabbed my hand and shook it. You might say I was startled. I couldn't figure out: why all this sudden courtesy?"

The officer introduced himself as Major Wainwright. He escorted the private into a briefing room and motioned toward a chair. Six other men, all older than he, all white, all in civilian clothes, already were seated.

A seventh man, in uniform, was standing. He introduced himself as Major William Coxe. Montgomery never saw him in uniform again. Then nodding at the seven men in civilian clothes, the major advised: "Gentlemen, meet each other." The introductions were brief, as it was made obvious that no names were to be exchanged.

Later one of the men was introduced as Colonel John Stephens. The others never were identified, although Montgomery learned they were from England, Australia and Canada and were astrologers. Today, Montgomery remains doubtful that the officers used their true names. He has been able to confirm the name of only one man he met at garrison, and that man, now an attorney in Jamaica, joined the group later.

After the strangely abbreviated introductions, Wainwright delivered what Montgomery recalls as "a brief speech" about the holocaust in Europe. He then came to his main point: The Germans were using especially gifted people—astrologers and psychics—to gain information vital to the war effort.

It was the first time Montgomery had ever heard the word "psychic." It was a few moments before he realized the officer was referring to the strange gift of clairvoyance he had possessed since childhood.

"Gentlemen, the six of you and myself have been selected to work with Military Intelligence, utilizing your particular abilities," the major remarked. The soldiers listened in silence, entranced. Not even a cough or the shuffle of a foot disturbed the quiet.

Wainwright then introduced Colonel Stephens. He stood and briefly traced the history of British Military Intelligence from the Norman Conquest in 1066 to 1943, when members of that elite corps were sending reports to Whitehall from around the world.

A psychic division of MI5 already was operating in Jamaica, he said. But it was necessary to expand it since more and more information from those with special abilities was needed for comparison and analysis.

"You will now be regarded as members of Military Intelligence . . ." Colonel Stephens paused. "Psychic Division."

Montgomery and the astrologers learned that G-1 was headquarters of the Caribbean section of British Intelligence.

The major explained that he had received authorization from the War Ministry to deputize them into Military Intelligence. The seven swore oaths of secrecy the first day and signed documents agreeing to maintain the oaths for twenty years or more after cessation of the war.

Private Montgomery was to continue his duties as a member of the band. Although his superiors at Upper Park Camp were not to know of his involvement with MI5, they were aware that he was to have privacy when needed and was to be available for calls from headquarters at any time.

Each of the men was given a code name. Montgomery's was "Jamaica."

He needed frequent time to himself. Naturally, his frequent absences from drill, and the special considerations he received soon led to a flurry of speculation and rumors among the other men. But Sergeant Major Rowe, Captain Scudamore, and another officer, assigned at Upper Park Camp to help with any special problems that might arise, helped him to sidestep major difficulties.

Montgomery's need for secrecy and his apparent position as "especially privileged" made it difficult for him to make close friends with other soldiers his age. He became the target of some jealousy and suspicion. Unavoidably, Montgomery became somewhat of a loner. Except for the time he spent on pass.

Six other Jamaican soldiers, all older than he, all with the military bearing and mien of career men, inexplicably attached themselves to him and became his new buddies when he went on pass. They watched over the young soldier as if he were a little brother.

When Private Montgomery donned his dress khakis and

headed for Kingston, two or more of his new friends went along. They were always with him. At chow time one of them would suddenly appear in line behind him. When he picked up a twelve-hour pass from Godfather, one or two of them would be waiting at the bus stop, also with a pass, and also headed for Kingston.

At first the youthful soldier was flattered by the attention from the older soldiers. They knew their way around. And they were big, husky men. Built like military police. In Kingston, among a sea of soldiers and sailors from all over the world ranging from Indian Sikhs to jaunty Australian paratroopers and dark-skinned Moroccans, the impeccably groomed men who accompanied him stood out.

It wasn't long before the excitement of all the attention from the older, more experienced soldiers began to wear off. There were times when a young guardsman didn't want the company of buddies.

Once, accompanied by two of his "companions," Private Montgomery struck out for Hanover Street. During and after World War II, Hanover Street had a dozen counterparts around the world: Hotel Street in Honolulu, Market Street in San Francisco and the Soho District in London. Girls, honky-tonks, booze and jukeboxes.

On Hanover Street a soldier could step in the J. Wray & Nephew Ltd. bar and buy a glass of rum for six cents. J. Wray & Nephew Ltd. owned one of the largest rum distilleries in Jamaica, and the company's bars were spotted throughout the island's cities and towns.

If gambling was on a soldier's mind he could usually find someone to help him put down a bet on that day's game of peaka peow. Peaka peow was a gambling game run by Jamaicans of Chinese descent. The game was played with dice, which the oriental bankers would throw until they came up with the series of numbers ultimately entered into large Chinese characters on a large board as the mark for the day. Couriers would spread out over the city, running from headquarters to barrooms, small stores and street corners with the winning number.

Most of the Jamaican working class played peaka peow, and

if they were lucky they could win as much as $200 for a six-cent investment.

In Kingston in 1943, hundreds of young women from the impoverished countryside congregated in the bars and hotels of Hanover Street. If you were a young soldier with coin in your pockets, a snappy uniform and pride in your manhood, and were looking for excitement, Hanover Street was where you wanted to go. But not with a pair of chaperones.

Yet even the massive influx of young women in the Hanover Street bars couldn't keep up with the number of soldiers from all over the world. There were still ten soldiers and sailors for every girl available. And those girls whose eye the private managed to catch were discouraged by the scowls of his burly companions. After several weeks he was getting desperate.

"I walked into the J. Wray & Nephew Ltd. bar on Hanover Street just below East Queen Street with two of my new friends and ordered a beer for each of us," Montgomery recalls. "Now, this was a place where a lot of girls stayed—night and day—and I was a young soldier. So I went up to the bar and ordered three bottles of Red Stripe beer. I took them back to our table and excused myself to go to the RR. I never came back."

Montgomery didn't see his companions until 11 P.M. at the Palace Theater, the main stop on the tram line back to the base, where they had agreed to rendezvous. One of the soldiers, his face creased into a scowl and his eyes compressed into slits, grumbled: "What, mon. Where you go?"

"I was taking care of business," Montgomery smiled. Then he skipped jauntily aboard the tram, trailed by two scowling, silent and unhappy companions.

The passes Montgomery was given and the business he took care of outside the base were infrequent and brief. To maintain his cover as an ordinary soldier, he had to keep up with all the drill and activities of his unit in the army band. He used what normally would be free time for other enlisted men in soul travel, meditation and briefing for his duties as a member of MI5.

Montgomery used two methods to obtain information, sometimes employing one to double-check the other.

The fastest and most accurate, but also the most debilitating was soul travel. Because of the strain on his already frail body this was generally reserved for emergencies or only the most vital missions—such as D-Day.

He calls the other method "Divine Revelation." It calls for him to focus his thought or to meditate on a particular problem and then to go to sleep. When he awakens, even after a sleep of only a few minutes, he usually but not always has the answer.

"The revelation does not come as a dream," he explains. "When I awaken, it's more like I have the memory of something. But it's usually the memory of something that is still going to happen. I just know it."

After the initial meeting, Montgomery seldom saw the astrologers, except for joint briefings and the occasions when he would meet them while he was at garrison to write reports.

At one of the joint briefings, Major Coxe introduced the group to a newcomer, whom he described as a good friend. The man's code name, Coxe explained, was "Spider."

Spider was an experienced MI5 agent who apparently worked as a psychic as well as with conventional methods of spying.

The team was given little more information about Spider. It wasn't until years later that Montgomery recognized him from a photograph as Ian Fleming, creator of the fictional James Bond series of spy thrillers.

Fleming, who died in 1964, served during the war as Personal Assistant to Britain's Director of Naval Intelligence.

He remained in Jamaica for about six months, apparently correlating and comparing the work of Montgomery and the astrologers and evaluating predictions.

Montgomery credits Fleming with inspiring more dedication within the unit by stressing the importance of its contribution to the war effort. He mentioned the work of the Nazi Occult Bureau. During one of the discussions he referred in person to "my predictions," indicating to Montgomery that he, Fleming, also was a psychic or astrologer.

MI5 officers called upon Montgomery perhaps twenty times during the three years for advice on specific events.

Once he was briefly assigned as bugler at a camp for German and Italian prisoners of war at Newcastle, Jamaica. Ostensibly his duties were to sound reveille and to perform other jobs of the camp bugler.

But his real mission, unknown even to the camp commander, was to check out rumors that prisoners were planning a break.

Although he could have performed his duties just as easily from the couch in Colonel Stephens' quarters, Montgomery was given a private room, where he went into soul travel to spy out the POW plans. What he learned was not very exciting, but interesting nonetheless. He found a conspiracy, all right. Two of them. But neither was especially threatening to the British authorities.

The Germans and Italians hated each other. In their quarreling, each was attempting to make it look as if the other group was planning a break. Consequently, the camp commandant was responding to reports by tightening security and removing privileges from both groups.

4

Hitler and the Occult

BLACK MAGIC, NECROMANCY, ASTROLOGY AND OTHER OC-
cult practices available for good or evil were deeply imbedded
in the National Socialism and leadership of Hitler's Third Reich.

Hitler, Hess, Himmler, Walter Schellenberg, Karl Haushofer and others among the masters of the Reich were practicing occultists and/or initiates of high orders in mystical
lodges.

Throughout Hitler's rise to power and during the war years,
the magical beliefs and pursuits of Germany's leaders guided the
destiny of the nation to a much greater degree than most people
realize.

Before World War 1, while still a youth, Hitler anticipated
the pursuits of the flower children of the 1960s, using psychedelic drugs to achieve levels of higher consciousness. At the
same time, he plunged deeply into the study of medieval magic
and occultism.

Adolf Hitler actively courted demonic possession. He used
his drug-induced awareness to guide him toward that goal and
toward personal power, according to author Trevor Ravenscroft
in *The Spear of Destiny*.[1]

Driven by this self-induced demonic possession, he and the inner-core leadership of the Nazi Party linked the occult weapons of the black magician with more conventional weapons of war in their assault against the Allies.

If nothing else, Hitler's miraculous escapes from assassination plots provide vivid proof that he was under the protection of dark forces.

In fact, there were seven or eight attempts made on Hitler's life, Dr. Montgomery learned. Each was doomed to failure because of the mysterious forces surrounding the Nazi leader.

When Montgomery went into soul travel to examine the Akashic records, the history of all time, he learned that Hitler was living a karmic pattern. The Führer could not be killed until his role had been played out and the demonic forces had deserted him.

During one expedition out of his body soon after he was recruited into the psychic division, Montgomery discovered a plot by several German officers who planted a bomb in an airplane Hitler was to fly from Hamburg to Düsseldorf to make a speech.

They devised an acid bomb, timed so that the acid would eat through the mechanism and then explode. But the protective cloud surrounding Hitler prevented the bomb from going off.

Another assassination attempt was thwarted in 1939, at the Munich Beer Cellar, where the Führer delivered a speech at an anniversary observance for the ill-fated Putsch of 1923, when the Nazis attempted to take over the government of Bavaria. He left minutes before a bomb exploded. This attempt figured prominently in the fate of the most famous astrologer of the Third Reich as we shall see later.

Black forces saved Hitler's life again near the end of the war, when two or three of his lieutenants tried to drop cyanide pellets through a vent, into his bunker. But the vents were built in a crisscross, up-and-down pattern, and the first two pellets dropped only a few feet. The fumes rose toward the conspirators, and they abandoned the attempt.

But the best-known death plot against the Führer was activated on July 20, 1944, by Staff Colonel Werner von Stauffenberg, as part of a plan to launch a military revolt and end the war. Von Stauffenberg placed a brief case loaded with explosives beneath the table during a meeting with Hitler. Unfortunately, a heavy table leg between Hitler and the bomb shielded him from the full destructive force of the blast. He escaped with only a burst eardrum and a hand injury.

Heinrich Himmler, Reichsführer SS, who worked with at least two personal astrologers, headed the Ahnenerbe, or Nazi Occult Bureau.

The Ahnenerbe incorporated membership of a mystical order founded by Aleister Crowley, a black magician from Britain, and two German groups—the Vril and the Thule Gesellschaft—into the black order of the SS.

Probably the most notorious and feared European occultist of the twentieth century, Crowley was a high initiate in Ordo Templi Orientis, a secret order with its parent lodge in Berlin. He also founded or worked with several other mystical organizations.

During World War I, Crowley journeyed to the United States, where he propagandized for the Germans, tore up what he claimed to be his passport at a public demonstration and wrote for *The Fatherland,* a pro-German newspaper. As a columnist, he penned virulent attacks against his homeland.

Several individuals held dual membership in the OTO and the Vril, a powerful secret lodge founded by Professor Karl Haushofer in Berlin. The Vril incorporated a worldwide membership dedicated to raising the magical consciousness of the Aryan race and to developing super powers.

The Thule Gesellschaft was a circle of occultists to which Hitler was introduced by Dietrich Eckhart, one of the seven founding members of the Nazi Party. The Thule group was the most powerful occult society in Germany. According to Ravenscroft, it was responsible for hundreds of murders, and much of the terrorist activity and race hatred that wracked prewar Germany.

In *The Spear of Destiny,* Ravenscroft writes that the German occultists sent expeditions to Tibet, where they contacted a group of satanic lamas whose ancestors fled to the Himalayas some time after the Great Flood described in the Bible. Eventually, the Germans imported a community of Tibetans to aid the Nazi cause.

Known as Initiates of Agarthi, they specialized in astral travel and were said to seek to inspire false leadership in all world civilizations. Hitler reportedly had regular conversations with their leader.

The adepts of Agarthi became known in Germany as "The Society of Green Men." They were later joined by seven members of "The Green Dragon Society" of Japan. The two groups reportedly had been in astral communication for centuries.

In the closing days of the war, Russian soldiers found their naked bodies in a suburb of Berlin. Neglected in the final months by the Nazis and facing the ignominy of capture by the Russians, they had committed ritualistic suicide with knife thrusts into the abdomen.

Earlier Himmler had established a school of occultism, and many of the leaders of the SS and Gestapo were ordered to attend courses in meditation, transcendentalism and magic. Thus the Ahnenerbe was used to incorporate membership of some Crowleyites, the Vril and the Thule Gesellschaft into the SS.

Ironically, in this atmosphere in which the core of the Nazi leadership was so deeply involved in occultism, occultists and astrologers outside the party vale were among the first victims of the widespread purges that shook Germany for fifteen years.

Hitler's birth date, April 20, 1889, led some of Germany's astrologers to fall into trouble early, when they pointed out that the man then rising to power possessed an unfortunate horoscope for a politician. Most destructive in his horoscope was the position of Saturn in the tenth house, which virtually assured him of an unfortunate end to his public career.

By the end of 1933, previously popular astrological weeklies and monthlies had been banned. A few years later, astrological conferences were being banned or put under surveillance by the Gestapo. Finally, astrologers and occultists not working for the Nazis were rounded up and sent to concentration camps, where many died.

The abortive flight to Scotland of Rudolf Hess, Hitler's designated heir and devoted follower, provided the excuse for the most severe and effective of the programs against astrology.

Among the Deputy Führer's staff at the Brown House in Munich was Ernst Schulte-Strathaus, officially an art expert, but better known to the Gestapo as an astrologer. Hess was also apparently involved with Karl N. Krafft, a Swiss astrologer and statistician.

Charges quickly were made that Hess had been under the influence of astrologers. As a result, the Nazis began rounding up amateurs and professionals. They confiscated astrological libraries and papers, as well as the stocks of books on astrology from publishers and booksellers.

Most of the people arrested were eventually released after signing agreements not to practice or discuss astrology. Some, including Krafft, were never released or were rearrested. He died on January 8, 1945, in Buchenwald.

Others like Elsbeth Ebertin, a graphologist turned astrologer, worked willingly for the Nazi leadership in Germany. Mrs. Ebertin died in an American air raid on Freiburg.

The puzzle of Hess's flight to Scotland has never been fully and satisfactorily explained by historians. Hess himself claimed that his only desire was to approach high British officials and arrange a peace treaty. Hitler, meanwhile, used his Propaganda Ministry to circulate the story that his deputy had gone mad.

Two years later, at the request of his superiors, Montgomery used his occult abilities to confirm that Hess legitimately was seeking peace and expected to be designated as new Chancellor of Germany. "He was a secret courier from Hitler, who believed he had ancestral links to British royalty," the psychic said.

Hess was carrying a secret letter, offering a separate peace, which Hitler planned to use to relieve his forces on the Western front so that they could turn on the Russians in the East.

"Of course, Hitler was planning a double cross," Montgomery reported. "But Hess was going to do some double-crossing of his own."

To demonstrate his good faith, the Deputy Führer turned over some German top secrets, including plans for Operation

Barbarossa, the attack on Russia. But his effort was futile, and he was imprisoned without an opportunity to speak to British leaders.

Sybil Leek, who later emigrated to the United States, was a girl in Britain at the time and played a key role in the Hess debacle.

"Ian Fleming came to me and suggested that I do a fake horoscope for Rudolf Hess. Ian told me that Hess was contemplating this trip to England and wanted a propitious day astrologically to make the trip."

Mrs. Leek, then eighteen, concedes that she was infatuated with the dashing Fleming and had a "love-hate relationship" with him, because she knew he was exploiting her abilities.

"He appealed to my patriotism when he asked me to do the horoscope. It was the one and only time I ever faked anything. I was horrified. But I did it."

Fleming delivered the horoscope to the unsuspecting Hess in Germany through a man he spoke of only as "a Swiss astrologer." Mrs. Leek believes the man was Krafft.

"Our code was to be: 'Hartz Mountain canaries sing better than any others,'" she recalls. It wasn't long before Mrs. Leek was advised that her imported German canaries were the best singers. Hess had made his historic flight and was in British custody.

Mrs. Leek, who made brief mention of the incident in her book *Astrological Guide to the Presidential Candidates*, admits to being consulted by several members of MI5 during the war years. But Fleming was her most frequent contact.[2]

In *The Occult and the Third Reich*, author Jean-Michel Angebert gives a slightly different perspective into Hess's flight. Angebert claims that Hess was carrying the British addresses of initiates of the Golden Dawn, as well as other highly placed Britons likely to look with favor upon his mission.[3]

Although the Deputy Führer's flight apparently hastened Krafft's imprisonment, it only activated a personal disaster that was fated for him regardless of the situation.

Krafft was an admirer of the Third Reich and initially worked willingly as a consultant for the Nazis, first making economic forecasts based on planetary cycles and major conjunctions and later forecasting about political warfare.

It was during this period in 1939 that he mailed a letter to a Nazi Intelligence official warning of alignments in Hitler's horoscope that showed the Führer's life would be in danger between November 7 and November 10. Soon after Hitler escaped the assassination attempt, on November 9, Krafft sent a telegram to Berlin warning that the danger would persist a few days longer. He was arrested for his trouble. Eventually it was determined that he had no connection with the bombing, and he was released.

Krafft's freedom was short-lived. Soon he was a prisoner again, this time working with Goebbels' Propaganda Ministry on the prophecies of Michael Nostradamus, sixteenth-century astrologist and seer. It was his job to interpret Nostradamus' predictions to show a final German victory.

A few years later with Krafft already imprisoned, De Wohl, Manolesco and other members of the British War Office Psychological Committee wrote new bogus predictions. Carefully worked out in the familiar quatrains of Nostradamus, they pointed to an eventual German defeat.

Thousands of leaflets carrying the new rhymed predictions were dropped over Germany. Negative horoscopes of Nazi leaders were also cast and dropped over Germany or smuggled into the Reich and occupied countries in German-language astrology magazines printed by the British.

While Krafft was vainly seeking his freedom, a well-known Hamburg astrologer, Wilhelm Wulff, was retained on the estate of Felix Kersten, a Finn and reputed White Magician, who had become a masseur and resident mystic to Himmler. Kersten was a pupil of Dr. Ko, a Chinese occultist, masseur and Tibetan-trained healer.

Under Dr. Ko's tutelage, Kersten mastered the healing techniques and became physician to the Dutch Royal Family before he was summoned as Himmler's personal masseur.

Kersten introduced Wulff to Himmler and to German counterespionage chief Walter Schellenberg. Himmler rapidly became dependent on Wulff's forecasts, and the astrologer found himself busy casting horoscopes not only of his Nazi bosses but also of Allied leaders including General Eisenhower, Field Marshal Montgomery and Churchill.

Wulff, like Krafft, worked in constant fear for his life, and quickly learned to couch some of the forecasts he produced in diplomatic secrecy.

Unlike Krafft, Wulff survived the war and lived to write the autobiographical *Zodiac and Swastika, How Astrology Guided Hitler's Germany* in an effort to clear himself of willingly collaborating with the Nazis.[4]

Goebbels too was greatly impressed by astrologers, and by mid-April 1945 just after the death of President Roosevelt and as the Reich was crumbling around its satanic masters, the propaganda chief sent for two horoscopes of Hitler and of the German Reich. Both had been carefully put together by the best astrologers in the Nazi Occult Bureau, and kept by Himmler in the research department of the Ahnenerbe.

Rereading the horoscopes, which had correctly predicted the outbreak of war in 1939, overwhelming victories, and then a series of disastrous defeats, the two Nazi leaders brightened when they read that an overwhelming German victory would occur in late April. It would be a victory so great, the stars had predicted, that a peace treaty favorable to Germany would be signed by August.

Less than ten days later Hitler and Goebbels were dead.

Noting that Hitler and Goebbels compared the horoscopes themselves, J. H. Brennan sagely observes in *The Occult Reich* that this is a feat they could not have accomplished without extensive technical training in astrology.[5]

Martin Bormann, Hitler's private secretary, loathed astrologers and always insisted publicly that the Führer had no interest in the occult sciences. But evidence indicates otherwise.

If the Nazi wedding to occultism contributed to the early victories, Hitler's later adherence to certain information gained through mystical/magical means, in place of the advice of his generals, likewise contributed to Germany's defeat.

The puzzling delay in development and employment of the destructive buzz bombs, which were unleashed on Britain only a few weeks after the invasion of Normandy, occurred because of a Hitler dream.

The Führer called a halt to V-2 rocket tests at Peenemünde after he dreamed, and then interpreted in trance, that if the rockets were fired they would damage layers of etheric formative forces around the earth, and a dreadful vengeance would be wreaked on all humanity—including Germans.

Hitler was finally persuaded that firing the missiles through the stratosphere would not disturb the etheric layer. But by that time, the opportunity to unleash the destructive new weapon on the concentration of troops and ships of the Normandy invasion force had passed.

Numerous other instances of the former World War I army corporal's interference with the military strategy of his generals have been recorded. Certainly, his actions must have often been precipitated by information gained from occult sources.

Dr. Montgomery's soul travel and meditation shed some light on why Hitler's reliance on occult powers worked so well in the early stages of the war and so poorly later.

During the final months of World War II, the only adviser Hitler would listen to was Goebbels, Montgomery says.

Initially, Montgomery found, Goebbels possessed certain psychic abilities. For some reason or another, however, they faded, and his advice turned bad. As Goebbels' psychic abilities soured, Hitler abandoned the advice of his other occultists and astrologers to rely instead on what evolved into nothing more than the opinions of his propaganda minister. The results were disastrous for Nazi Germany.

Of course, very different results occurred while Hitler was listening to his astrologers, the Tibetan masters and his own as yet unmuddled psychic impressions.

Brennan states unequivocally that Himmler was a necromancer who had boasted to Kersten of calling up spirits and conversing with them. Like Hitler, Himmler was a trained magician, rather than a natural psychic.

Most of those individuals close to Hitler had some experience in the occult.

Hermann Göring, head of the Nazi Luftwaffe, for a time the

second most powerful man in the Reich, was less involved than
most of his fellows in Hitler's court. But even Göring became a
member of the Edelweiss Society in 1921 while he was in
Sweden. The society was an offshoot of the Golden Dawn and
taught the concept of a coming Nordic messiah. Göring also
believed strongly in reincarnation and claimed to have once
been the Roman emperor Tiberius.

Ironically, another man who followed Hitler's initiation into
black occultism from close range and who had frequent contact
with him early in his political and mystical career lived to become one of his greatest nemeses.

He was Dr. Walter Johannes Stein, a Viennese scientist and
scholar of the occult. Dr. Stein spied on Hitler and the Third
Reich with both occult and conventional means. According to
Ravenscroft, who studied history under him for twelve years,
Stein confidentially advised Churchill during World War II
about the workings of the minds and the motivations of Nazi
leaders.

Stein was able to observe the rise of Hitler and the National
Socialists at close range until 1933, when he was forced to flee
Germany because Himmler had ordered his arrest. Himmler in-
tended to press him into service with the Nazi Occult Bureau.

It was Dr. Stein, Ravenscroft says, who as a British Intelligence agent, brought plans to Whitehall for the Nazi invasion of
Britain. Whether the information was obtained by occult or conventional means is not mentioned.

Hitler's failure to order "Operation Sea Lion," the invasion
of Britain, into action immediately after the evacuation of
Dunkirk, when his forces were at their strongest, is one of the
most puzzling aspects of the war.

One answer is occultism, this time employed by Britons, although by no means by anyone connected with the War Office
or Whitehall.

Witchcraft in the British Isles never was completely
stamped out by the Church during the terrible persecutions of
the Middle Ages. It just went underground.

During the war and postwar years, with the attention of the
world on other things, Gerald B. Gardner, a Scotsman, practicing

nudist, retired customs officer and occultist, brought Witchcraft back into the open. The publicity Gardner generated led other Witches to begin coming out of the closet and was instrumental in the revival of the religion on both sides of the Atlantic.

But Gardner credited himself with an even more impressive accomplishment. English Witches, he claimed, prevented the invasion. They raised a cone of power and directed thought forms at Hitler, telling him that he could not invade English shores.

The feat has since become legendary among the growing numbers of followers of the Old Religion, who recall that a similar gathering of Witches was convened before the defeat of the Spanish Armada.

Some Witches who participated in the ritual against Hitler were so exhausted and depleted of energy that they died shortly afterward.

A few years ago, when Gardner first disclosed the incident, the story could have been expected to bring general grunts of disbelief. But today, when parapsychologists are taking such things seriously as psychokinesis, astral and soul travel, photography of auras or energy fields around the bodies of animals and plants and an astronaut communicates with earth from outer space via ESP, can it continue to be laughed off?

No one has come up with a better explanation. It appears that Hitler could have ordered the first invasion of England since 1066, and might very well have been successful. Yet, inexplicably, he abandoned the plan.

It should be clear that British Intelligence and the High Command, including Churchill himself, were aware of the black magical and initiatory practices in the Third Reich. The British were equally aware of the value of sensitives and adepts, friendly to the Allied cause.

5

Soul Traveler

ASTRAL PROJECTION: THE ABILITY TO SEND ONE'S ETHERIC body forth from the physical body to travel on the material and astral planes.

Soul travel: The ability to project one's soul or the non-material replica of the physical body to journey through any or all planes of existence. Soul travelers journey not only on the physical and astral planes, but on higher spiritual levels, closer to the ultimate cosmic force.

Millenniums before the advent of rockets and the atomic bomb, ages before the threat of humanity annihilating itself with world war, the ability to project one's etheric twin from the physical body fascinated men of ancient Egypt, Israel and India. Even St. Paul makes reference to it in II Corinthians:

> I knew a man in Christ above fourteen years ago (whether in the body I cannot tell; or whether out of the body, I cannot tell: God knoweth); such a one caught up in the third heaven. How that he was caught up into paradise, and heard unspeakable words, which it is not lawful for man to utter.

The long history of the Catholic Church lists many miracles in which the soul mysteriously leaves the body, wanders to other realms and then returns. St. Anthony of Padua and St. Alphonsus Liguori each sent their astral essences forth as they lay in church chapels. Their astral bodies were seen elsewhere as they rested, seemingly dead.

In the East, out-of-body experience plays a major role in Anahat Yoga, Sufism and Lamaism. Guru Nānak, founder of the Sikh sect, was adept at dispatching his soul at will. He left detailed written records of his journeys.

Indeed, the theory of soul and body transcends all religions, with the belief that at death, the two parts separate, with the physical remaining and the spiritual traveling on, whether it be to heaven, Valhalla or any of the other myriad terms used for the Great Beyond.

After the birth of Christ, Plutarch related the story of a soldier who fell unconscious and wandered on other planes for three days. Nearly two thousand years later, American writer Mark Twain was astonished to see a man approach him and then suddenly disappear. He reported the incident to a nineteenth-century center for psychic research.

In *The Astral Journey: Evidence for Out-of-Body Experiences from Socrates to the ESP Laboratory,* Herbert B. Greenhouse relates how Ernest Hemingway experienced momentary astral projection while working with an ambulance unit during World War I. He was attending to a group of Italian soldiers, when a mortar shell exploded nearby.

"I felt my soul or something coming right out of my body, like you'd pull a silk handkerchief out of a pocket by one corner. It flew around and then came back and went in again, and I wasn't dead anymore," Hemingway stated. He later used the incident in *A Farewell to Arms.*[1]

Aldous Huxley was at writer D. H. Lawrence's side when the latter was dying. Lawrence told Huxley how he had seen his astral double leave his body and stand in a corner of the room.

The first Western group established to study the phenomenon was the British Society for Psychical Research, founded in 1882. Four years later, investigators including psychiatrist William James, Sir Oliver Lodge and others compiled their findings in *Phantasms of the Living,* a large volume that detailed accounts of the living—and dead—appearing to relatives and friends.

Today, in the United States, the work continues at such major centers as the Psychical Research Foundation, Durham, North Carolina; the American Society for Psychical Research, New York; and Stanford Research Institute, Menlo Park, California.

Now associated with the University of California, at Davis, Dr. Charles Tart began testing out-of-body experiences at the Psychical Research Foundation several years ago. His most startling case involved Robert Monroe, a Virginia businessman, who related his experiences in *Journeys Out of the Body.* Tart recorded Monroe's travels with the use of electroencephalographs and other devices, as well as assigning subjects tasks to perform while out of their bodies.[2]

Tart was quoted by writer Alan Vaughan in an article in *Probe The Unknown* magazine as saying that out-of-body experiences convince astral travelers of life after death. They know there is survival after physical death, because they have been there, Tart maintained.[3]

One of the most amazing substantiated out-of-body experiences tested, occurred at SRI, where physicists Harold Puthoff and Russell Targ conducted experiments with psychic artist Ingo Swann. Swann was uncanny at describing the locales of distant points on the globe after projecting out-of-body and journeying to precise longitudinal and latitudinal co-ordinates stipulated by the researchers.

Once, they supplied him with the co-ordinates of what they believed to be the center of Lake Victoria, Africa. When Swann returned to his body, he told the researchers he had flown over water and then stopped on dry land. When Targ and Puthoff informed him that he had to be wrong, Swann was adamant. Later, the researchers checked their maps and discovered that they had directed the psychic to a peninsula that jutted into the lake.

The late Sri Paul Twitchell, a modern founder of ECKANKAR, a worldwide religious cult, was probably the best-known exponent of soul travel in the Western world, before his death. Sri Darwin Gross succeeded him as leader of the religion, whose followers use soul travel as a means of reaching SUG-MAD, or the Godhead.

"The basic principle of soul travel is that man is the spirit self, that he can take charge of the soul body and can move from the visible planes into the invisible worlds at will," Twitchell wrote in *ECKANKAR, the Key to Secret Worlds.* "When he becomes proficient at this, the beneficial results are freedom, clarity and wisdom."[4]

For years, Twitchell studied the spiritual teachings of the East while formulating his religious beliefs. He speaks of Rebazar Tarzs, a Tibetan adept and great teacher, who taught that the individual must free himself from focusing his attention inside his body to project his soul.

Means of exiting the body vary widely and may include trance, dance, shock and sleep or dreams.

Sri Twitchell taught that: "In the uninitiated, or those who have no knowledge of soul travel, the soul generally leaves at the solar plexus, or the stomach area. For those using the astral technique, the soul leaves at the pineal gland, or what is called the spiritual eye. The other places for the soul to leave the body are the back of the head, called the oblong medulla; the thousand-petaled lotus, as it is called by the Hindu teachers, or what we know as the pituitary gland at the center of the head, and last, the heart center, known to the Hindus as the *Anahata.*"

When Ernesto Montgomery left his body for the first time, it was quite by accident. He was eleven years old and living on Beeston Street in Kingston. Like many other island children, he often played hide-and-seek after dark. In Jamaica, however, the game included an important twist: whenever a child hid, he was supposed to invent a tall story about where he had been. Those who were not found by the others within an allotted time told their stories, and the one with the best tale won.

A long row of brick steps led to Ernesto's Beeston Street apartment. Underneath, there was an empty space, large enough for children to hide under. One time Ernesto ran to the steps and curled up in a corner underneath.

"Of course, you stay still, so they don't find you. I went into

a particular corner and started to think up my story. Suddenly,"
he recalled, "I felt myself riding in a car. We were going along
the railroad track. Before we got to the track, I told the driver
exactly where we were, even though I had never been in that
section before." An instant later he was lifted up. Light and free,
he felt himself levitated above his surroundings.

The noise created by other youngsters trying to find him
brought Montgomery back into his body with a slight electrical
jolt. It was years before he realized that he had been soul
traveling.

Even though the first out-of-body experience is traumatic or
frightening to many people, for young Ernesto it was also an extremely beautiful sensation.

"I got frightened afterwards. But I felt as if I were floating
and could look down on earth and see everybody. It was a feeling of complete joy, happiness and contentment. People I met
just floated, as if floating on clouds. You walk, but float. It is like
paradise.

"I would say that these people I saw were spirits of the departed, not others soul traveling. There were so many of them,
and everyone looked so happy."

On the soul plane other souls look like ordinary people, but
they are surrounded by what appears to be a puff of smoke, he
learned. "It looks like what one would envision for the Garden
of Eden: trees constantly blooming, plentiful fruit, sparkling
pools and streams of water. There is no apparent racial
difference among the souls. They are just one universal group of
people without color."

Looking down upon men and women on the earth plane, he
saw that each individual had two bodies. "It's like when you see
a shadow. The soul-travel side is the side of positivity. One fol-
lows the other. It looks like a double image. I saw this. Later, I
was able to see that every person has the potential to make soul
travels."

But he became aware of a certain danger that awaits those
who leave their bodies. The astral plane is so filled with peace
and contentment that if the traveler remains there too long, he
can lose the desire to rejoin his physical body.

"After fifteen minutes, I have an overwhelming urge to remain," Montgomery admits. "If you don't return in time, you can damage your physical body. That is why today there are so many people in mental institutions. I have read of astronauts who tell of looking down on the earth from the moon. They exclaim about the beauty of the stratosphere. That is exactly what we see when we are out of the body.

"There are very few souls who wish to return, because soul travel is the cousin of death. Many students of metaphysics, yoga, Buddhism and other religions and sciences go into deep meditation and never return. I would say many of the younger students have committed suicide. My teaching is that young students should never go into any kind of deep meditation, which can put them in the realm of either soul or astral travel if they are not alert how to return."

An Ann Arbor, Michigan, yoga instructor who was found dead in June 1975 could have been one of those who was unable to return, Dr. Montgomery believes. Robert Antoszczyk, twenty-nine, was in near perfect health before going into his bedroom to meditate. Friends said he left instructions that he did not want to be disturbed because he was going to attempt astral projection.

Four days later his lifeless body was found on the bed in his room, his thumbs turned between his index and middle fingers. It is a position that yogis use for deep meditation.

Dr. Paul Gikas, University of Michigan pathology professor, theorized that Antoszczyk may have gone into deep trance, slowing his heart to such a degree that his brain no longer received sufficient blood to sustain life.

Dhamapati M, a spokesman for the Integral Yoga Institute, was quoted in news stories as saying that Antoszczyk must have been inexperienced, because if one can project to the astral plane one can return. That is not always true, Montgomery believes, because the soul body doesn't always want to return.

"If you don't return in time, your physical body can also be possessed by negative entities. There are so many waiting. I personally will not take any chances. I can project my body very capably for fifteen minutes, possibly two hours. But the beauty of it, the desire not to return, is what convinces me to return within fifteen minutes. I protect myself with meditation and deep thought."

During World War II, psychic spy Ernesto Montgomery frequently resorted to trance or soul travel to gather information about the enemy. Several times, he encountered the astral forms of German spies on similar missions. He met the etheric bodies of many men in the Nazi hierarchy, including Joachim von Ribbentrop, Heinrich Himmler, Joseph Goebbels, even Hitler himself.

He also learned that the Nazi command was rent with jealousy, bitter quarreling and backstabbing.

It was on the astral plane that the Jamaican soul traveler met a woman he remembers vaguely as "Anna Schwegel, or something like that," and a man whose name he did not know. The German mystics were psychic spies for the Nazis.

"Fräulein Schwegel" was a heavyset old woman who had the stern appearance of a devoted mystic. She had risen to a high rank in Hitler's psychic division.[5] The man, who may have been twenty years her junior, was perceived by Montgomery to be a zealous Nazi, yet more of a statesman than his fellow astral traveler. Their relationship with their Jamaican counterpart, in the peaceful atmosphere of the astral plane, was a friendly one.

Souls meeting each other on the astral plane or on yet higher levels of existence hold no animosity toward others on any plane, even though they may be on a mission such as those undertaken by the psychic spies on both sides during World War II.

"When I met them on the astral, we were always pleased to see each other," he recalls. "The fact that I was working for the British and they were working for the Germans was not important to our relationship there."

The psychics, Jamaican and German, communicated telepathically. "We would look at each other and understand. It was a rather outstanding, beautiful experience."

The teen-age psychic's lone meeting with Adolf Hitler on the astral plane was not a beautiful experience. The Führer's soul was much more subdued in the etheric body than the physical body. And even on the peaceful astral plane, the Nazi leader projected an air of uneasiness and apprehension.

Hitler was an intelligent man who developed a universal hate and a deep commitment to the black arts, and his etheric body was different than any other that Montgomery had met. It was withdrawn. If other souls were in the area, Hitler's stayed at a distance by itself.

"The other souls were friendly and tried to evolve in a manner that would make the physical life worthwhile. But Hitler's was separate and apart from everything.

"He was not the type of person you would want to strike up an acquaintance with. By his conduct on the astral plane, he showed what kind of soul he was. Hitler was a reincarnation of Judas Iscariot, who betrayed Christ. In this reincarnation, he did not change from that kind of character. He came back as a villain."

Hitler did not glow like other souls of either the departed or the living, that the psychic spy encountered. Hitler's soul had a glum, sullen appearance, a claylike complexion. "You could see that he was surrounded by evil. His entire intent was to inflict suffering upon the world."

Montgomery did not witness Hitler's physical death in the closing days of the war, but he knows the generally accepted story of the Nazi leader's death by suicide to be true. Soon after the fighting ended in Europe, Montgomery went into trance. He saw Hitler and his newly married wife, Eva, swallow cyanide. Hitler fired a bullet into his head. A small revolver dropped unfired from Frau Hitler's hand, as she died.

Later, still in trance, the young soldier-spy watched as Frau Goebbels and a doctor murdered her six children. She then joined her gnomish husband in suicide.

During the hostilities, Montgomery used his powers to determine the strength of air divisions, to follow German Field Marshal Rommel in Africa and Allied generals Patton and Montgomery in Europe. He was able to pinpoint the location of Axis ships and submarines. He foresaw the defeat of the Japanese in Asia.

Even at his lowest point of physical strength, when he was projecting daily to protect the Normandy invasion, he never had trouble returning to his fatigue-wracked physical body after ten or fifteen minutes on the astral plane. Almost a quarter of a century later, however, an error in judgment almost cost him his life.

The year was 1971, and a woman traveled from San Diego to Los Angeles, seeking Montgomery's help. She had just learned from relatives that her mother was dying in Fort Worth, Texas. Before flying to Texas, she wanted the psychic to determine if the report was true, and if so, to perform a healing.

Dr. Montgomery was reluctant to interfere. The older woman was in her seventies, and apparently reconciled to crossing into the spirit world. "But no daughter or son will accept the fact that the Bible tells us we are supposed to be here only three score and ten years," he says, "so I finally agreed to see what I could do."

He had frequently soul traveled great distances to apply his healing techniques to the ill. In this instance he promised only to project and observe the physical condition of the old woman to determine if she could be helped, and if she wanted to be helped.

Although he had projected without assistance hundreds of times, he was uneasy about undertaking the mission without an experienced helper present. The San Diego woman was not familiar with the dangers of soul travel, or skilled in any field of medicine.

Nevertheless, he finally stretched out on a couch and went into deep meditation, after instructing her to pour cold water on his legs to shock him back into his body if he didn't return in fifteen minutes. He told her to pay special attention to his breathing, which would indicate trouble if it became erratic or labored. In moments, his soul had lifted from his body, unseen by the woman in his office.

She saw only that the psychic's body had suddenly taken on the look of a corpse. His breathing slowed to near imperceptibility, and his normally dark flesh faded to an ashen color. Panicking, she ran from the office.

Montgomery's soul body, meanwhile, was with the old woman in Fort Worth. She had lumbago, arthritis, inflammation of the joints and a chronic heart condition. The psychic applied healing power to ease her discomfort. Then he projected back to his Los Angeles office and to the physical body he had left lying so quietly.

His soul hovered over the physical body, ready to return. But somehow, the soul was blocked. It was unable to slip back into the sheath of the physical form. The woman he had left there was gone.

It was nearly forty-five minutes after he had first projected, that a friend found his still form on the office couch. He called for an ambulance, which rushed the psychic healer to a hospital. Doctors took one look at him and said he was dead. But a closer examination disclosed a weak pulse, and he was given oxygen. The shock from the sudden rush of oxygen permitted his soul to slip back into his body.

The shaken psychic was hospitalized for three weeks. He was drained of energy and had severe pain in the left side of his chest. Several doctors were consulted, and when x-rays disclosed trouble with his left lung, two physicians recommended removing it. Others disagreed, and there was no surgery.

With the help of the doctors and his own healing powers, Montgomery's health mended. He vowed never again to undertake soul travel without a trustworthy aide nearby if he was not completely at ease about the projection. He would project again, many times, without assistance. But he would never again ignore warnings of uneasiness or doubt.

Early in 1975, Montgomery was asked by *The National Tattler*, a weekly family newspaper, to soul travel to the bedside of ailing Greek shipping tycoon Ari Onassis. Rumors about the critical state of Onassis' health had been prevalent for six months. Montgomery reported:

> I observed that Mr. Onassis is in a more advanced stage of illness than the press reports had indicated. It was necessary that he have the use of oxygen, and he was being cared for by a very concerned staff of six specialists and four nurses.

Unfortunately, I have the impression he will succumb within four months. There appears to be no cure.[6]

Thirteen days after the newspaper appeared on the stands, Onassis was dead. Once more, Dr. Ernesto Montgomery's uncanny psychic abilities had been proven true.

6

Psychic Spies and the Iron Curtain

EARLY IN 1945 MEMBERS OF MI5's PSYCHIC UNIT IN Jamaica began to turn some of their attention from the Germans to Russia, Britain's powerful ally to the east.

American, British and Russian troops already had smashed their way across German borders and were pressing the defenders on two fronts. It was only a matter of time before the German resistance would crumble completely.

The Russian Army had slashed mercilessly through the retreating German Wehrmacht on the Eastern front and was demanding that Britain and the United States stand by and allow it to become the sole conqueror of Berlin.

The uneasy alliance among the United States and Britain on one side and Russia on the other was showing signs of strain, as the Allies sensed the kill. It did not require the clairvoyance of a psychic to foresee the years of hostility ahead between the Soviet Union and the Western powers. Experienced diplomats already were growing uneasy at the prospect of postwar political dealings with the intransigent Russians.

But Allied political leaders had met and agreed to the division of Germany into occupied zones. Berlin was in the eastern zone, allotted to the Soviets, but as the traditional capital of the defeated nation it would also be divided. Corridors of entry through the Russian territory were supposedly assured by political agreement.

The young Jamaican psychic was unsophisticated in the machinations of world politics, but he was ready in late March when his superiors in MI5 directed him to look into the future of the postwar relationship of Britain, the U.S. and the U.S.S.R.

For weeks Private Montgomery had been receiving ominous warnings of trouble ahead between the Western super powers and Russia during his nightly meditations. The Russian bear and international Communism quickly would replace the Nazi swastika as the chief threat to world peace, he foresaw.

Now at the direction of Majors Wainwright and Coxe, he retired once more to the officers' dayroom to delve further into the problem of Anglo/Soviet postwar relations, by trance and divine revelation.

When Major Wainwright awakened him a short time later, his expression was clouded. In a vivid dream, he had seen the British union jack, the American stars and stripes, and the red hammer and sickle of the Soviets afloat in muddy water. Smaller flags of lesser powers surrounded them.

The flags drifted apart, the Soviet banner and those of Poland, Czechoslovakia, Hungary and other East European nations moving away from the others.

Even to the politically naïve island youth, the interpretation was obvious. The deep distrust between the nations soon would become open enmity.

Strong forces were at work dividing Russia from its former partners in the war against the Axis. A division, he told the two officers, was unavoidable.

Through free will and by taking firm, bold action immediately, he advised, the Anglo-Americans could add immeasurable strength to their postwar position.

Although much of what occurs is fated and cannot be changed, many other things may be altered or avoided by conscious effort and action of man, he explained. "We must try our best to gain as much territory as possible," he urged.

As previously mentioned, the division of territories already had been agreed upon, unknown to the psychic—and probably to the two intelligence officers. The Anglo-American zone was to be about two hundred miles west of Berlin, putting the German capital deep inside Soviet territory.

Yet the capture of Berlin would carry with it considerable distinction and respect. Its capture conceivably could be influential in later negotiations among the Allies.

By the last week of March, Eisenhower's forces were still three hundred miles from Berlin. The Soviets had advanced to the Oder River, and their lead units were thirty miles from the German capital. Eisenhower had determined to leave Berlin to the Russians and had notified Soviet Premier Joseph Stalin that his troops would seek other objectives. It was less than a week after Private Montgomery's dream vision of the muddy flags.

Churchill was furious. He angrily complained that Eisenhower should direct British Field Marshal Bernard L. Montgomery to make a run for Berlin and to support him with all the American strength available. The Prime Minister pointed out that at that stage of the war military maneuvers had now taken on important political significance.

After an exchange of communications with the combined chief of staff of the Western Allies, as supreme commander of the forces in the field, Eisenhower continued with his plan. Russian troops were the first to enter Berlin.

Dr. Montgomery has no doubt today that the information he obtained through divine revelation was an important factor in Churchill's last-minute effort to deny Berlin to the Russians.

Churchill was not the only Allied political leader who was impressed by the potential military and intelligence value of sensitives. "Stalin and Field Marshal Timoshenko, I believe it was, listened intently to whatever information came out of Jamaica," Montgomery says. "I was made aware of this by MI5, and I also confirmed it through my own psychic insight."

Some of the most famous mystics in history have come from Russia: Grigori Rasputin, Madame Blavatsky and George Gurdjieff.

Stalin, to be sure, must have known at least some of the history of these world-famous mages. But it was a Jewish refugee from Poland, fleeing certain death at the hands of the Nazis, who captured his imagination and interest during World War II.

The story of Wolf Messing, who carried a 200,000-mark price on his head after making a public prediction that Hitler would die if he invaded the East, is recounted in *Psychic Discoveries Behind the Iron Curtain*.

As recounted by authors Sheila Ostrander and Lynn Schroeder, Messing was arrested and beaten soon after the fall of Poland. But using his powers of will he caused all the German officers and guards to leave him and congregate briefly in another room, giving him time and an opportunity to slip away. He fled to Russia.

His reputation soon brought him to the attention of Stalin, who ordered a unique command performance. The Soviet dictator ordered the Polish refugee to rob a Moscow bank, using only his reputed ability to project his will telepathically into the mind of the teller.

Watched by two witnesses designated by Stalin, Messing walked up to an elderly cashier, handed him a blank piece of notepaper and slid an open attaché case onto the counter. He willed the cashier to give him 100,000 rubles. The old man handed the money over.

Messing showed the rubles to the two witnesses and then with their concurrence returned the money and blank paper to the cashier. The old man dropped to the floor with a heart attack. Messing later related in his autobiography, *About Myself*, that the attack was not fatal. Stalin was impressed. But he wanted more proof.

At the dictator's direction, the psychic was next taken to a government building and left in a room. Three sets of guards were ordered not to let him leave either the room or the building. In minutes he was outside, waving at an official watching from a window.

More impressive yet was the time Messing was told to enter Stalin's dacha at Kuntsevo without a pass or any documents indicating he had permission to be in the closely guarded hideaway. Platoons of guards watched the house, and all of Stalin's servants were secret police.

Messing sauntered into the dacha, walked past the guards and servants without incident and stopped in the doorway of a room where Stalin was reading. Messing, who had curly dark hair, explained to the astonished Soviet dictator that he accomplished his feat by implanting the idea in the minds of the guards and servants that he was Lavrenti Beria. Beria, the dreaded head of the Soviet Secret Police, was bald, wore a pince-nez and was well known to the staff of the dacha.

There is no mention in Messing's autobiography of his being required by Soviet leaders to use his talents for military purposes or for internal or external spying. But as Ostrander and Schroeder say: "One wonders if Stalin ever put Messing to more practical, political use."[1]

Dr. Montgomery says the Soviets used the talents of various psychics during World War II. So it seems likely that Messing was called on for more than mere test demonstrations of his incredible abilities. Some information from Russian and British psychics was pooled for a time, Montgomery recalls. In view of the vivid demonstrations Messing provided, the Russian leader obviously had good reason to consider more practical use of the Polish sensitive's astonishing abilities.

Any interest the Russians may have had during World War II in using sensitives for military or intelligence purposes did not die with Stalin. At the very least the Soviets today are experimenting seriously with the use of psychics for these purposes.

According to Ostrander and Schroeder, in 1963 the Kremlin gave top priority to the biological sciences, including parapsychology.

"Major impetus behind the Soviet drive to harness ESP was said to come from the Soviet military and the Soviet Secret Police," they wrote. "Today the Soviet Union has some 20 or more centers for the study of the paranormal with an annual budget estimated in 1967 at 12 to 20 million rubles ($13 million to $21 million)."[2]

The Soviets used submarines for experiments with ESP at least as early as the mid-1960s. If not sponsored by the military, which they may have been, the experiments would at least have had to be carried on with the full cognizance and support of the Soviet Navy. Rabbits were used to gauge the ability to communicate telepathically. The military usages of such a breakthrough are obvious when one considers the restrictions on conventional communication methods between submarines and other vessels or shore installations. Radio is useless.

ESP experiments aboard submarines, it would seem, confirm military involvement.

Ostrander and Schroeder say they have seen confidential Western reports on military institutes in the U.S.S.R. where ESP research is being done. The Russians, they say, are attempting to train clairvoyants for use as spies.

This confirms warnings of Dr. Montgomery, who says psychic spies have been working for the Soviets for several years. In two or three years, psychic spying by the Soviets will be perfected and so sophisticated that conventional methods of espionage will be needed only to confirm and supplement information gathering by occult means.

"Russian diplomats are going to be picked from among the best psychics in the Soviet Union," he cautions. "They won't need cameras, microfilm . . . all those dramatic implements that Fleming wrote about in his books. All they will have to do, is the same thing that I do. Lie down, project their thoughts or go into soul travel. Then walk away with all the information they want."

If the American government shares Dr. Montgomery's concern, it has been coy about admitting it. Official Washington does not volunteer information linking the field of parapsychology with military and intelligence matters.

Ironically, reputed experiments aboard the American nuclear submarine *Nautilus*, reported by French journalists in 1959, are credited with sparking a reawakening among Soviet scientists of the military and intelligence potential of parapsychology.

On the basis of journalistic speculation that the Americans were on the verge of perfecting telepathy as a new atomic age military weapon, Soviet science plunged back into the field of parapsychology after a slowdown in interest for a decade or more.

The U. S. Navy denied and is still denying the experiments. The Pentagon, in fact, all of official Washington, is reluctant to discuss involvement in the field of parapsychology. There are indications, however, that official Washington is very much aware of the potential in these fields for the effective use of sensitives.

Dr. Andrija Puharich, of Ossining, New York, was called to Washington with other parapsychologists in 1952 to discuss the possible uses of ESP, telepathy and other unconventional means of gaining information for use by military intelligence.

In an article, "Can Telepathy Penetrate the Iron Curtain?" in the Winter 1957 issue of *Tomorrow*, Puharich had written that it could.

The effects of Israeli Uri Geller's psychic powers on metal have been under study at the U. S. Naval Ordnance Laboratories.

Geller was observed in other experiments at the prestigious Stanford Research Institute by George Lawrence of the Pentagon's Advanced Research Projects Agency and by Ray Hyman, a professor of psychology with the University of Oregon. Hyman frequently has been consulted by the Defense Department.

Other government agencies also have shown an interest in American psychics.

Ted Serios, probably the most tested psychic in the United States, was warned away from a trip to Russia by a government agent.

A former Chicago elevator operator and an alcoholic, Serios has the ability to take psychic pictures of objects thousands of miles away by balancing a Polaroid camera on his knee and facing the lens. Unfortunately, control of the images he gets has been negligible. He might be concentrating on a kidnap victim and get a picture of the Eiffel Tower. Even this of course is no mean feat for someone sitting in a laboratory in Colorado.

The Chicago psychic submitted to laboratory experiments under the direction of Dr. Jule Eisenbud, associate clinical professor of psychiatry at the University of Colorado Medical School for more than a decade.

"They've fed me truth serum, liquor, marijuana, speed, all

kinds of stuff to see if I could get pictures when I was using it— whatever it was," Serios says.

After a few years of experiments, Serios tired of the life of a laboratory rat. When he was invited to Russia to meet some scientists there, he quickly agreed to the trip.

Serios was having a drink on a flight to Chicago from Denver when a man sat down next to him, identified himself as a federal agent and started talking about the trip to Russia.

"He knew who I was and he knew about the trip to Russia," Serios recalls. "He said he didn't think that it was a good idea for me to go, although the government couldn't really stop me. 'But once you're in Russia, you know, we're not responsible for you,' he said."

Serios did not go to Russia.

He later teamed up with an old friend, psychic Joe DeLouise, also of Chicago. The two psychics wanted to work for the government and in 1975 attempted unsuccessfully to contact officials in Washington.

Dr. Montgomery agrees that psychics and federal agencies, especially but not exclusively those in the Pentagon, should work together. Clairvoyants are not only being trained as spies in Communist bloc nations, he says, but dormant psychic powers are being developed in potential espionage agents who have not previously shown evidence of psychic abilities.

Dr. Milan Ryzl, a Czechoslovakian-born parapsychologist who emigrated to the U.S. in the early 1960s has successfully activated psychism in persons who previously had no inkling that they possessed those abilities. The same thing can be done in this country, Montgomery insists.

"The Russians and the British have accepted psychism, and the American government and the scientific community here are going to have to accept these gifted people for what they are," he says.

PART 2

The Police Years

1

The Clairvoyant and the Criminal

VJ DAY, THE VICTORY OVER JAPAN, ENDED PRIVATE Montgomery's career with the Jamaican Home Guard and British Intelligence.

There was a brief thank-you from Major Wainwright and a reminder that the oath of secrecy would be binding for twenty years, or longer, if considered in the best interest of Great Britain. The Jamaican branch of the intelligence network was disbanded.

In October 1945, less than two months after the end of the war, Montgomery was demobilized and handed an honorable discharge.

He had played a significant role in the Allies' defeat of Fascism, but a role that only he and a handful of others knew about. And he was under a vow of secrecy not to discuss his exploits with others.

Anxious to show its appreciation to the men who had served it so well, Great Britain offered members of the Home Guard their choice of a demobilization bonus, land in Jamaica or educational benefits. Twenty years old, with no job, no family and very much aware that from now on he would be completely on his own, Montgomery chose education.

Immediately he signed up as a student at Kingston Technical School, where he took courses in typing, shorthand and speech.

The next problem he had to face was getting a job. Although his demobilization benefits paid school tuition and some of his living expenses, the money would not be coming in forever. So Montgomery became a clerk with the Jamaica Postal Department.

Sorting letters, filling in for ill routemen, and riding bicycles from one pickup box to the next was not a job that the former British Intelligence agent picked. It was the one available.

There was no way he could use his experience of the past thirty months as a psychic spy to obtain more exciting employment. At the time, he had no desire to use his psychism professionally. He had had enough of that for a while. In the past, it had only disrupted his life, making him a veritable fugitive in his childhood and a virtual prisoner unable to leave the base without bodyguards during his army career.

No, he was determined that his psychic abilities would stay in his past.

Montgomery did not miss using his psychic powers, but he did miss his uniform. Uniforms and marching bands always have appealed to him. And the sound of "Semper Fidelis," "Georgia" or "The Washington Post March" can always be counted on to bring him running, regardless of what he has been doing or how important his business may be.

He was not working with the postal department long before he was accepted as a member of the Jamaica Special Constabulary, an auxiliary police force that trained evenings and was available for mobilization in time of emergency. Once a member of the JSC, Montgomery lived solely for the evenings.

By now, he had completed his work at Kingston Technical School. Feeling the spiritual pull of his early religious training once more, he attended night classes at West Indies Baptist Seminary at his own expense. His nights were divided between classes at the seminary and drill with the JSC.

He was outstanding in both. Once back in uniform his enthusiasm for the JSC was so obvious and his performance so good that superiors recommended him for appointment to the regular police department.

Carrying a letter of introduction from Deputy Commissioner Sanguenetti of the Special Constabulary Department, Montgomery was given entrance tests. He passed and soon was a rookie constable patrolman.

After training, he was assigned to a station in Spanish Town, about sixty miles from Kingston. It was there that his psychism caught up with him again.

Constable Montgomery developed the unnerving habit of telling his fellow officers the disposition of court cases they were involved in before the cases were heard.

And more than once, he grabbed a fellow officer and took off on the run to break up a crime that had not yet occurred. The word circulated fast that Constable Montgomery was "different."

One day in 1952, Constable Clementson, a close friend of the psychic-policeman, was to testify against a woman he had arrested for possession of marijuana. A conviction automatically meant six months in jail, with no probation or suspended sentence.

"In Jamaica," Montgomery recalls, "the law is like this: If you have two ounces of ganja, it is six months in jail. If you have 100 pounds of ganja, it is six months in jail. If it is your first offense, you go to jail. So the question before the judge is: 'Was the person guilty?' If the answer is 'yes,' that person go to jail. There was no such thing in Jamaica at that time as a suspended sentence."

Consequently, the defendant showed up with Barrister Norman Washington Manley, one of the best attorneys in the island.

Clementson was not impressed by the reputation of the attorney. The constable had a good case. He had picked up the woman, and then, after she was in custody, caught her attempting to drop a bag of ganja down a toilet.

"Mon, you are going to lose," Montgomery told his friend.

Two hours later the woman walked out of the courtroom with her attorney, smiling at a not-guilty verdict.

Clementson walked out soured, but a wiser policeman.

He had testified that he had taken the woman to the lavatory, turned his back and then swung around quickly—in time to see the reflex action of her hand after she tossed the ganja into the open pit. He said he recovered the drug from a shelf just inside the lavatory.

But when he was asked during cross-examination by Manley if he had seen the woman actually take the marijuana from her dress or bosom to toss into the pit, Clementson had to admit he had not. A. C. V. Graham, resident magistrate for the Parish of St. Catherine, ruled in favor of the defendant.

Soon, other officers were checking in with Constable Montgomery before they testified in important cases, to determine what the outcome would be.

"Well, the young man is going to get six months in jail," Montgomery might tell one. Or, "He is going to get off." Or, "She is going to get away, and sue you."

Montgomery's friends did not always like his predictions. But he was always right.

One night while riding a bicycle on patrol with his partner, a district constable, Montgomery suddenly said:

"Let's turn right here and go left, mon. A man steal a goat."

"What?" his startled companion asked.

"He is down there, mon," Montgomery insisted, pointing. "A goat thief is down there. Let's turn and see what happen."

The district constable had been on patrol with Montgomery before and did not argue. The two officers turned their bicycles right, pedaled a few feet and swung a sharp left.

A youth, about sixteen years old, was struggling with a goat. He had the animal's head in an armlock. With his other hand, he was viciously twisting its tail.

The two policemen jumped off their bicycles, tossed them against the wall of a building in the narrow street and grabbed the surprised youth by the shirt. "Where did you get the goat?" they demanded.

The youth released the armlock he had on the animal's head, and freed his other hand from its tail. "Aw . . . Corpie," he pleaded, turning his palms upward in supplication, "gimme a chance?"

A magistrate gave the goat thief three months in jail, instead, time to mull over the hard hearts of Jamaican police and to figure out what had gone wrong.

Most of the crimes Montgomery worked against in those days were similar small offenses, such as stealing goats, chickens, another man's bananas or raising, selling or possessing ganja.

There was violent crime, of course, but it usually was confined to the stabbing or hacking of a husband, wife or friend with a machete during a family quarrel or after drinking too much of the cheap domestic rum. When a murder or serious assault occurred, there was usually little mystery involved. And once he was sober, the suspect generally went quietly with the police to face the consequences.

Admittedly, in Jamaica as nearly everywhere else today, people have changed. Even the easygoing Jamaicans have not escaped the armed robberies, shootings, rapes and violent crime so common in the rest of the world.

In the late 1940s and 1950s, when Montgomery was a constable in Spanish Town and Kingston, officers were armed only with their clubs or batons, except for special emergencies or on night patrol in the very worst sections.

Two of those sections were the west portion of Spanish Town Road in Kingston and an area behind Coronation Market, called "Dung Hill." Dung Hill was where the Rastafarians squatted in little huts. Police could not go in Dung Hill, day or night, unarmed or armed.

Officers pursuing a thief, ganja dealer or anyone else they suspected of a crime, stopped at the market. Once the suspect reached Dung Hill, he was safe—from police if not from his fellows—until he ventured out again.

Police stationed at the Smith Village Police station, nearest the market and Dung Hill, always were armed.

There were other hazardous sections where policemen were better off not to venture alone, including Pinnacle, a high area in St. Catherine Parish between Spanish Town and Kingston, which was known for its excellent ganja.

One evening as Montgomery was off duty and stretched out alone on his bunk in his nightly meditation period at the Ferry Police post in St. Catherine Parish just before dropping off to sleep, he found his inner vision focused on an immense field of ganja. Vibrations from Spanish Town Road and Pinnacle were pulling at him. His meditations were through for that night.

Montgomery leaped from his bunk, slipped quickly into his uniform and bicycled to Caymanas Village, where Mayo Holcomb, a friend, owned a small shop. The excited policeman told Holcomb about his vision, and the two began to walk toward Pinnacle.

At a point not far from the village, Montgomery followed his vibrations, left the road and continued walking overland. Holcomb followed. The men had walked about five miles when they came to a clearing.

There, illuminated by the moon and with its four-foot stalks waving in the ocean breeze, was the biggest field of ganja Montgomery had ever seen. "There was ganja everywhere. No trees, no bushes, just ganja."

The two men pulled a pair of plants, and Montgomery returned to the Ferry Police station, reported his find and showed the evidence to the corporal.

Early the next evening, Montgomery and the corporal had checked out guns and were hiding in bushes at the edge of the field after reporting to divisional headquarters in Spanish Town that they were going on patrol. It was another moonlit night. The men waited. The silence was broken only by their own breathing, the sound of insects, the occasional call of a night bird or the rustling of a mongoose or other small animal as it moved through the underbrush.

It was about 4 A.M. and the ground mist was heavy, hugging the tops of the marijuana plants in a wispy blue blanket before the two policemen heard footsteps and the low murmur of muted voices.

Four dark forms materialized from a row of coconut trees a hundred yards to their right, two men and two women. They entered the field. Machetes tucked in belts that held up their ragged pants, the men began chopping at the caked earth around the roots of the plants with hoes. The women followed behind, sprinkling water from cans.

The two policemen watched the pastoral scene for a few moments. Then, at a signal from the corporal, they leaped from their hiding places yelling:

"You are all under arrest. We have guns. Drop everything."

The women screamed. The hoes and watering cans hit the ground with a clatter, and four pairs of hands were reaching in the air. The officers advised them to take their machetes from their belts and drop them to the ground. They did, carefully easing them and letting them drop point first into the dirt.

Montgomery and the corporal gathered three big bundles of marijuana plants, passed them on to their prisoners and began the five-mile walk to the road. There was a surprise waiting for them at 8 A.M., when they walked into the village behind their prisoners.

The street was filled with more than a hundred people, many of them policemen.

The two officers had reported the night before that they were going on a four-hour patrol. Constable McKenzie, the station guard and their immediate superior, had alerted divisional headquarters in Spanish Town at 2 A.M., after their patrol had stretched to six hours. More than seventy policemen and JSCs had been called out to search for them. They need not have worried.

Young Constable Montgomery had a closer brush with danger when violence broke out between two warring political parties in 1953, and he and another officer were caught in the middle.

Montgomery was on duty in Spanish Town that day. As he walked his beat, he was thinking of a political picnic and rally that was to be staged in a few hours by the Jamaica Labour Party, JLP.

Suddenly, he stopped in his tracks. In the street ahead of him, the images of bodies formed, undulating in the shimmering heat. The two-wheeled wagon of a fruit vendor was tipped onto its side. The guavas, mangoes, melons and breadfruit that spilled out were smashed under the feet of men and women, whose faces were contorted with hatred as they rushed at a line of police, screaming and throwing rocks and bottles. The policemen, crouching behind wicker riot shields, defended themselves with tear gas and clubs.

Montgomery took a step backwards and closed his fist over the baton at his belt, ready to join the fray.

In an instant, the mob was gone. Ahead of him there was only the dusty street and the few souls whose work or responsibilities required that they be out during the hottest part of the day.

The young officer had experienced visions before, and the meaning of the brief glimpse into the future was clear. There was going to be a riot in Spanish Town. Soon. So when he saw a fellow constable, Officer Burton, approaching on a motorcycle, Montgomery flagged him down.

"We should have some help here, mon," said Montgomery. "There is going to be a riot, and it will be too big for us to handle."

Burton, whose fellow policemen knew him better as "Sabu," because of his round face colored the hue of coffee with cream, laughed. "You are crazy," he said. "Nobody riots in Spanish Town. It is too hot, and besides, what's the use?"

Montgomery persisted. And he was specific. "Go for help," he insisted. "By four hours, the Labourites and the PNPites [People's National Party] will be rioting."

Sabu laughed and roared away on his motorcycle, kicking up a cloud of dust around Montgomery's feet as he went.

Four hours later Spanish Town was under siege, Montgomery had been roughed up, he had made the only arrest he ever regretted, and Burton's motorcycle was wrecked.

Rum was cheap in Jamaica in those days. Six cents would buy a glassful of white rum. That day, rum and politics proved to be a combustible combination.

Jamaicans were looking forward eagerly to independence, and emotions between supporters of the two major political parties were high. So, when a large group of JLP Kingstonians showed up in Spanish Town for the rally later that night, it did

not take too many glasses of the potent white rum to set the fire-
works off.

The fight started in a tavern and spilled out into the street,
almost at the feet of Constable Montgomery. He stepped in to
break it up and arrested a PNPite who was kicking his fallen op-
ponent. A moment later, a huge dock worker's fist landed on the
constable's jaw and Montgomery was sprawled on his back. The
dock worker aimed a kick at the policeman's ribs but before he
could land the blow he was swung around and punched in the
face by a Kingstonian. That was the signal, and a dozen men
leaped at each other. Forgotten for the moment, Montgomery
scrambled to his feet and ran for help.

The first policeman he saw was Burton. Burton may not
have been the most diplomatic constable on the police department, but he was no coward. He knew that if the full-scale riot
Montgomery had predicted was to be avoided, the fight would
have to be broken up immediately. He rode his motorcycle into
the scramble of bodies.

Arms and legs thrashing wildly, Burton lost sight of his
wrecked motorcycle just before a half-dozen yelling laborers
tossed him into a ravine.

It was a subdued and bedraggled police constable, his clothing in tatters, his face, arms and legs scratched and punctured
from brush and stones, who dragged himself back to the police
station behind Montgomery.

Police sounded a riot alert, and officers streamed into
Spanish Town from Kingston and other communities as the
crowd grew and the violence increased. Police were issued tear
gas and loaded rifles. As the rioting grew in force, the police
began to launch the tear gas canisters at the mob. The gas further infuriated the rioters.

Montgomery was barely on the street again before he found
himself backed against a wall with two companions, holding his
rifle barrel down with one hand and batting away flying rocks
with the other, as the crowd charged them. A heavy woman was
in front, the sweat streaming down her face as she screamed,
waved her arms and ran directly at Montgomery. There was a

wall of shouting men and women behind her, hurling rocks and shaking fists and clubs.

Reinforcements arrived on the run and a phalanx of policemen closed in on the crowd from both sides, just as the woman reached Montgomery. The young constable leaped, clamping a headlock on her. Quickly and expertly, he shifted his weight and jerked her arms behind her, slapping his handcuffs onto her wrists.

She screamed curses at him all the way to the station. There, he tried to calm her down long enough to explain that she was under arrest for rioting.

"That is when she told me that she was not rioting," he recalled. "The other people were rioting. She was a Labourite from Spanish Town, and they were Kingstonians, PNPs, and they were chasing her with stones. She was running to me for help. That was one mad woman."

Strikes vied with rioting to keep police busy, as Jamaicans lived through the agonizing birth pains that preceded establishment of a new national government, moving from the status of a colony to that of an independent member of the British Commonwealth.

As in many Caribbean, South and Central American nations, the United Fruit Company was a major landowner and employer. It was sometimes appreciated, and sometimes—when attacked and accused of exploiting the people of the island—it was not.

When the Jamaica Labour Party called a strike against United Fruit at Lluidas Vale in St. Catherine Parish during a struggle for bargaining rights at the huge plantation, constables from the Half Way Tree Station, Bogwalk Ferry and Spanish Town were called to help keep order. Montgomery was stationed at Spanish Town.

At the sugar estate, the police were billeted in laborers' barracks. Montgomery was stretched out on a blanket on the floor next to his helmet, gas mask and rifle one night meditating, when suddenly he picked up a danger signal. Scrambling to his feet and grabbing his equipment, he yelled to his friend Clementson that there was trouble at the factory.

Clementson didn't argue. He grabbed his helmet and rifle and dashed out the door after Montgomery. The factory was about a hundred yards away, quiet and dark against the moonlit sky. As the policemen rushed inside, two men were sloshing gasoline onto machinery used for crushing sugarcane into pulp so that the juice can be extracted for distillation into molasses and rum. The gasoline cans clattered to the ground as the men yelped and ran through the deserted building. They escaped out a rear door.

Arson was common practice and an effective weapon of strikers during labor trouble at the big sugar estates. This time the psychism of Constable Montgomery was more effective.

Nineteen-fifty-three was a tempestuous year in Jamaica. It was the same year that Montgomery was assigned to guard Alexander Bustamante, when the Jamaican patriot and founder of the Jamaica Labour Party led his supporters to Spanish Town for an election to determine bargaining rights at the Caymanas Sugar Estate in St. Catherine Parish.

Because of the volatile nature of the times and the high emotions between the contending JLPs and the PNPs, Constable Montgomery was instructed to stay with Bustamante every minute of his twenty-four-hour stay at the sugar plantation.

Montgomery stuck to the political leader like his shadow, his gangling form dogging the steps of the bigger man as the little group of JLPs and their bodyguard trekked from polling place to polling place.

As they approached a tent, Montgomery leaped past Bustamante and sprinted for the back of the canvas structure. Two men jumped in alarm as he yelled. They dropped the wooden ballot box they were stealing and hurdled across a gully, sprinting away. By this time, followed by Bustamante's younger companions, Montgomery bounded after them. The men were collared by Montgomery and his JLP helpers.

Capture of the two suspects and return of the ballots helped explain Montgomery's action in disobeying orders and temporarily deserting Bustamante. His superiors were not surprised. By this time, they were used to the young officer's sudden hunches that always were right. Word about Constable Montgomery's strange abilities was getting around. Eventually, it reached Kingston.

Constable Montgomery was transferred to the capital. There, he met Andrew P. Locke.

Locke was a former British paratrooper who headed a special branch of the Jamaica Constabulary Force. The division included an internal investigation branch, a group which worked with the Immigration Department, and a section to infiltrate and investigate radical movements.

"Mr. Locke called me to his office, and we had a long conversation," Montgomery recalls. "Then he pointed out that he was a paratrooper during the war and that he knew of certain people who served Military Intelligence in a special psychic branch."

Montgomery had been sworn to secrecy. He kept his mouth shut about his wartime experiences, but he did concede that he had a local reputation as a psychic.

Locke assigned him to internal investigation. As Montgomery was turning to leave, his superior officer remarked that he might call on him "sometime" for psychic advice.

Being assigned to the internal investigation unit did not mean that Montgomery would be able to forget foot patrol duties and other assignments provided for the lower ranks in the police department. Instead, he continued to carry out those assignments and was trained in fingerprinting and other identification techniques, as well, in order to develop a cover for his primary job.

He had to work harder than before. He had to keep up two jobs—one as a cover for his real assignment. But on the surface there was little difference in his work. In Kingston, young Constable Montgomery was working harder than he had in Spanish Town.

One night, he was assigned duty on King Street and was standing next to a closed dry goods store during a heavy rain. Clouds filled the skies, covering the stars. The only light came from the headlamps of one or two bicycles that had passed during his late night tour of duty.

He was wearing his night uniform: black tunic, black trousers, black shoes, black helmet. Except for the shiny gold belt buckle on his uniform, everything—including the constable—was black.

The young constable was startled when a man suddenly appeared next to him and pushed a key against his gleaming belt buckle.

But he was not nearly as startled as the stranger was seconds later when the constable realized what was going on and reached down to clamp his hand around the man's neck.

"I can still hear that man scream, and he throw the key, I don't know how far," Montgomery remembers. "He was a thief, and everything was so black that he thought my belt buckle was the lock on the door. It was a frightful surprise when he tried to push in the key and I grab him."

Montgomery is convinced the man was an amateur, because professional burglars at that time usually entered through the roofs.

Despite his slight build, Montgomery rarely had trouble when he was making an arrest. Police were given unarmed self-defense instructions during basic training. More important, most Jamaicans respected the police and submitted to arrest without struggle when caught breaking a law.

There were a few occasions, however, such as during the rioting in Spanish Town, when Constable Montgomery had to defend himself from angered men or women he was trying to arrest. But it was not the arrest of a Jamaican—it was the arrest of a British sailor that nearly cost Montgomery one of his hands.

He was on foot patrol on a Friday night in 1955 in an area near the docks, when he observed a drunken sailor staggering along the street.

"Every woman that passed him, he would grab at her breasts," Montgomery says. "So I arrested him for indecent assault, being drunk and disorderly conduct."

The use of handcuffs on a suspect picked up for a minor crime was optional, and Montgomery and other constables often merely advised the individual that he was under arrest and then clamped their right hands around the left wrist of the offender.

This is what Montgomery did with the sailor. A moment after his hand closed over the wrist, the sailor jerked his arm down, twisted and sunk his thumb into the soft metacarpal bone of Montgomery's hand. Then he bent the constable's fingers back.

The metacarpal splintered and separated. Montgomery recoiled in pain, grabbing his injured hand.

The sailor pulled away and headed for a group of companions nearby. Montgomery was right behind him. The injured hand was useless, but he grabbed the sailor by the blouse with the other and was fighting a losing battle, when a passing cabdriver jumped into the fray. Between the two of them, they subdued the unruly seaman, pushed him into the cab and took him to jail.

Montgomery's troubles with the hand were just starting. By the next morning, it had swollen to twice its size. By Sunday, it was so big, he couldn't pull his short-sleeve shirt over it when he dressed to go to the public hospital. The hospital was closed.

It was Monday before doctors saw the hand for the first time at the University Hospital and put it in a cast.

It was too late. When Montgomery returned three weeks later, x-rays disclosed the bones were not knitting. They were still splintered and jagged. Worse yet, he had contracted gangrene. The chief surgeon told the police constable that the hand might have to be removed to prevent the poison from reaching his heart.

Montgomery asked for a week to try to save his hand. Reluctantly, the doctors agreed. They loaded him with penicillin and sent him home.

Until that time Montgomery never had thought about doing a self-healing. But now it was obvious that if the hand was going to be saved, he would have to use the strange powers that had so plagued and benefited him in the past. He began a week-long period of concentrated meditation.

"I did not visualize the gangrene, because that was negative. That is what I wanted purged," he explains. "Instead, I removed the cause of the trouble by visualizing the entire hand whole and fit."

Illness and injury, Dr. Montgomery says, are so closely related to the subconscious that positive thinking can often prevent disease, hasten healing and cure.

"Illness or whatever it is is too often a condition of the mind," he says. "Your mind can make you sick. And your mind can make you well."

"A person can constantly be thinking, 'I have a back pain every morning at nine,' or, 'I have cancer,' or, 'I have lumbago,' and through this thought in a couple of months you can go to a doctor, and you have the condition you have been worrying about. Your mind makes it manifest."

Proper visualization can be a powerful method of healing. Of course, charismatic healing—healing through the direct power of God and the Holy Spirit—is yet another approach Dr. Montgomery uses. This will be discussed at greater length in another chapter.

When Montgomery returned to the hospital one week later, the ugly purple streaks that had previously revealed the blood poisoning in his hand and arm were gone. Swelling in the hand itself had diminished.

Doctors agreed that the hand was much improved. In a week, the infection had cleared, and the blood was cleansing itself. It would not be necessary to amputate, but they did operate to remove the bone splinters and about an inch-and-a-half section of the damaged metacarpal.

The operation left Montgomery with a stiffened hand, which kept him off normal duty for nearly a year. It was unlikely, the doctors told him, that he would ever regain normal use.

Montgomery resumed meditation and prayer. For nearly a year, he prayed and meditated daily, visualizing a normal hand. Slowly the stiffness faded, and the use of his fingers returned. Today, except for a depression at the top, where the section of bone was removed, the hand is normal.

2

A Meeting with Winston Churchill

ERNESTO MONTGOMERY DID NOT TRAVEL TO GREAT BRITAIN during World War II, but his reputation and exploits as a psychic spy evidently did. Through top secret channels, his name reached Prime Minister Winston Churchill at 10 Downing Street, in London.

"Long before he came to Jamaica in 1945, I learned that he had been following my career for years," Montgomery says. "He was of the opinion that my work was invaluable to the war effort."

But by the fall of 1945, the black psychic no longer was an operative for MI5; he was a member of the band of the Jamaica National Constabulary Force. Churchill was changed, too. He and the Conservative Party that he led had experienced a shocking defeat at the hands of the Labourites. When the portly statesman visited Kingston that year, he was a dejected, rejected, embittered and depressed man.

The former Prime Minister told Montgomery that he always had been interested in the "unknown."

"Churchill wouldn't dismiss any area of the occult, but he especially liked the logic of astrology," maintains Sybil Leek, who was better known during World War II as an astrologer, rather than as one of the world's foremost Witches, as she is today.

"You could show him a chart, and he liked this. It was something he could see. On the other hand, to him, psychic impressions seemed more like something that was plucked from thin air. Churchill liked facts."

Extrasensory perception (ESP) and the predictions of psychics played a more important part in Churchill's life, according to Count Manolesco.

"Earl Winterton said to me jokingly one time: 'Do you know, Churchill believes very strongly in psychics, but he doesn't believe in astrologers?' Whether or not he believed in our work, I don't know. But he didn't like us; I know that.

"One day, I happened to show the Prime Minister his personal horoscope and urged him to slow down his drinking. He was very angry and said to me: 'Get out of here, you bastard!' He could be very nasty.

"But Churchill accepted graphology, palmistry and other things. For some reason, however, he didn't like astrology. And it's too bad," Manolesco says. "His birthday was November 30, which made him a seventh-degree Sagittarian, and he could have been a good astrologer himself."

Even as Adolf Hitler was protected by dark forces and survived so many attempts on his life, Churchill also was protected by ESP or occult foreknowledge of disaster on several occasions. Other times, it provided him with key insights about the enemy and war.

In *My Early Life*, Churchill's autobiography, he told how he had acted in a subconscious manner to find his way to the only house occupied by a British sympathizer in a certain part of South Africa after escaping from imprisonment in the 1899 Boer War.

During World War I, even when his most important military decision, the invasion of Gallipoli, went against the British, his psychic powers provided the concept of the armored tank. And by 1917, he had envisioned a landing craft capable of bringing tanks from ship to shore. This transport vessel came into being more than thirty years later, when the Allies used floating harbors to launch the Normandy invasion.

In the early stages of World War II, with the Germans capturing mile after mile of Free Europe, Churchill's intuitive powers told him that he had to see Louis de Wohl, then interned as an enemy alien in London and about to be shipped to a camp in Canada even though his heritage was Austrian and Swiss.

The request mystified Churchill's staff, since the Prime Minister could not have had any knowledge of the incarcerated, would-be "potential spy." Immediately, however, they arranged transportation for the prisoner to the Downing Street address.

Unseen forces had informed the Prime Minister that Louis de Wohl was to be an important man in the war effort. Somehow, even though his file on the man failed to show it, Churchill knew De Wohl was a highly regarded astrologer. In fact, he was the author of several reliable books on the subject.

The moment De Wohl arrived at the Prime Minister's home that day in 1940, all fears he might have had about imprisonment in North America ended. As soon as he entered Churchill's office, the cigar-smoking leader asked him if he could supply day-to-day, hour-to-hour astrological charts of Hitler's life. Prior intelligence already had revealed that the Führer relied heavily on his own chart readers to interpret the stars and plot his life.

Churchill could not have chosen a better man for the job, he quickly learned. Years before, in peacetime, De Wohl had known Jan Erik Hanussen, Hitler's first astrologer, and knew his system well. Although Hanussen was killed in 1934 and other men had become Hitler's astrologers, the system was basically the same.

Immediately, the Prime Minister ordered an office and staff to be put at De Wohl's disposal. For the remainder of the conflict, the astrologer provided invaluable information about Hitler's probable military strategy and political moves.

"Sir Winston was a genius," De Wohl once said. "He followed many hunches and, for one reason or another, these feelings he had were usually right. He had a sixth sense, a psychic inclination, of which only a few people knew."

Weeks before Churchill met De Wohl for the first fateful

time, that "sixth sense" saved the Prime Minister's life. He was climbing into the rear seat of his chauffeur-driven limousine when he suddenly changed his mind and walked to the other side of the car. He took the seat directly behind the driver, a position he never had occupied before.

Minutes later, as the limousine sped down the highway, a German bomb exploded beneath the seat where he sat. But with Churchill's weight squarely over the explosion, the car remained upright and miraculously stayed on the road.

Later, Churchill explained his decision: "Something in me said: 'Stop. Go around to the other side, and get in there.'"

In October 1940, shortly after his first encounter with De Wohl, Churchill's intuition saved the lives of several members of his personal staff. With a German blitz beginning just as he sat down to dine, he suddenly got the impression that the kitchen of his Downing Street home soon would be struck, killing anyone nearby. But he knew that this time, at least, he would be safe.

He was enjoying a pre-meal glass of champagne when he received the intuitive warning. Suddenly sirens wailed. He rose from the dining table, darted to the kitchen, ordered servants to bring out his food on hot plates and then to go immediately to nearby bomb shelters. His dinner, at least, would not wait.

Churchill then resumed his seat in the next room only a few yards away and freshened his glass. Moments later, the building rocked from a nearby explosion. An aide rushed in to inform the Prime Minister that the pantry and kitchen had been destroyed and another portion of the building damaged.

"Somehow, I knew it was coming," he mused. "But I'm glad no one was injured."

Churchill's occult powers saved his life once more on April 13, 1942, when he decided not to attend a military air show at Wiltshire as previously scheduled. Something told him to postpone his visit until the next day. He sent Brigadier Grant Taylor in his place.

Unfortunately for Taylor, he would not live to see the conclusion of the low-level-attack exercise planned for the afternoon. In a fatal human error, a Hurricane fighter plane swept down on the field and opened fire on the review stand instead of dummy soldiers and vehicles laid out nearby.

Taylor died instantly along with twenty-six other men. Sixty-eight more were wounded.

The day after the tragedy, Churchill kept his promise. He sat where Taylor had died twenty-four hours before. The demonstration went off without further incident.

As much as the Prime Minister's intuitive powers or subconscious use of the occult helped him throughout the European conflict, however, they did little to perpetuate his political career once Berlin finally fell.

It had been ten years since the last general election in the British Isles, and Churchill realized his people favored another referendum. With Hitler defeated, he was sure voters would demonstrate their confidence in him by returning the Conservative Party to power.

Even as the war in the Pacific continued, on May 25, 1945, Churchill dissolved his coalition government in favor of a caretaker Conservative regime. Three weeks later, he dissolved the House of Commons and announced elections for July 5.

There was little time for Clement Attlee, the Labour leader, to marshal his forces, and a Churchill victory appeared imminent, even in the eyes of his foes. But he quickly lost votes by branding a possible Labour Party victory as "the beginning of a Communist takeover in Europe."

"During the war, he had been a national hero," stated Victor L. Albjerg in his book *Winston Churchill*. "In the election, he stooped to partisan hack. Throughout the war, his speeches had rung with exemplary eloquence and grandeur. In the election campaign, a good many of them were ordinary harangues.

"Likewise, his former enthusiasm for Mussolini and Franco exacted a price in electoral votes. His addiction to imperialism, even in imperial England, by 1945 had become a political liability, since most Englishmen had lost the Edwardian enthusiasm for empire and its advocates."[1]

More problems for the Prime Minister arose because his Conservative Party and the coalition government in general had protected the rights and insured the interests of nobility and gentry during the ten years it was in power, Albjerg said. What few benefits the working classes had received from Parliament were token by comparison.

The election came, and so did defeat. Churchill took the people's verdict hard: "It would have been better to have been killed in an airplane accident or to have died like Roosevelt," he said. "No sooner was the peril over, than they turned me out."[2]

Only days after the former Prime Minister tendered his official resignation to the Crown, King George VI attempted to show his gratitude by offering him the Order of the Garter.

"I could not accept the Order of the Garter from my sovereign when I had received the order of the boot from his people," Churchill replied.[3]

He still had not recovered from the shock by late 1945, when he made the Atlantic crossing to Jamaica, where he met Montgomery.

The frail black psychic-policeman was nervous as he made his way to King's House that bright fall day. It was one thing for him to enter into a trance or go into astral travel to gather information about the war. But it was quite a different matter for him to meet the recently deposed head of the British Commonwealth.

Once before, when Montgomery still was a member of the Jamaican Home Guard, Sir Anthony Eden came to the island. But even though Eden was a great statesman, he was still a decade away from Downing Street.

"I was stationed at Mona when Eden came," Montgomery recalls. "We talked in the office of Lieutenant Parkinson, my company commander. We called him 'Parkie.'

"At the time, Eden was only a member of Parliament. We talked for about a half-hour, but just in generalities. I didn't make any predictions for him. I think he just wanted to see what I looked like. A lot of these people who came to Jamaica did that.

"Sir Anthony was very vague. He asked me how I liked the army, how I liked my job. Of course, I was still doing very secret work, so he didn't even indicate that he knew I was a psychic. I figured that out, because I certainly wasn't the best soldier, just the best drummer on the field.

"I figured he had some inkling, and this is definitely why he met me. I was in uniform. And I never performed my psychic chores for the army when in military dress. I marched in, snapped to attention and saluted. He asked me to relax and to sit down. It was a rule that when people came to see me, no one else would be in the room."

Eden was a prominent politician, it is true. But Churchill was almost a god. The uneasiness Montgomery felt, heightened as he walked across the King's House lawn for the meeting with the great man.

It took him only a few seconds to clear the standard security force on station and to pass on to Churchill's personal guard. Seconds later, he entered a small drawing room fitted with table and chairs and came face to face with the former Prime Minister. Churchill immediately tried to put him at ease.

"He was a rather unusual man," Montgomery recalls. "He said to be seated, and we just started to talk. He was smoking a cigar and was talking from the corner of his mouth, like a ventriloquist. He was calm, cool and collected, completely in charge of the situation.

"But I was able to detect that he was easily riled and sometimes would fly into rages. He did this when he started talking about the ungratefulness of his people, his British people. He flew into a rage, but calmed himself immediately."

Churchill possessed the ability to speak about an unlimited amount of subjects knowledgeably, Montgomery says. "He never missed a point. He talked about the United States, politics and his boyhood. He just rattled from thought to thought.

"He talked of 'the knowledge of the unknown,' as he called it. He seldom used the word 'psychic' in the hour or so we met. He tried not to let on that he knew more about the occult than he admitted. But he did tell me he practiced projection, knew dream interpretation and psychism.

"He must have been a student of the occult to know so much. Later, I learned that he was using his own psychic ability in the House of Parliament to see what he could come up with during the war.

"Later, through my own methods, I was able to learn that he used a great deal of mind control in his work during the war, as well as information he was receiving from Free France, Britain and other countries which had psychics working for them.

"During our conversation, he dispatched two cigars and smoked the first one completely out. It was strange, but the ash from the first cigar didn't drop at all. He showed me why it hadn't. He had put a small bit of wire in the middle of the cigar, and this allowed the ash to stand still, although only ash.

"I asked him why he did this, and Churchill replied: 'It is one of the ways I test the people I meet the first time, to see how observant they are.' We both had a laugh at that. He said he picked the trick up from his friend Sir Artie Shawcross, a leading British lawyer."

The former Prime Minister was a master at getting the man before him to relax. But to Montgomery, the meeting was nevertheless somewhat of a confrontation between a "Commander-in-chief and a raw recruit." He was worried about the way he worded his sentences, uncomfortable about his youth. Despite the other man's friendly attitude, he still was aware of his station and maintained a degree of regimentation in his response.

Churchill did not speak about his family, only of himself. He was concerned about his future and asked the psychic to use his powers of clairvoyance for him.

It did not take long for Montgomery to see that the former Prime Minister would be returned to power. It would not be long before the Conservative Party regained control of Britain once more, he said. And when it did, Churchill would move back into 10 Downing Street.

Churchill was delighted when the seer predicted that once more, the British sovereign would offer him the precious Order of the Garter, the oldest form of knighthood in Europe. This time, Montgomery said, knighthood would not be refused.

The portly statesman left the psychic's company somewhat relieved, the depression he felt from his defeat partially removed.

Soon after, Churchill returned to top political form. He embarked on a speaking tour of the United States, and on March 5, 1946, at Westminster College, Fulton, Missouri, uttered words that left their mark on history. Again, he criticized the Communist takeover of Europe and its threat to the Free World. This time, however, his warning was listened to with respect.

"A shadow has fallen upon the scene so lately lighted by the Allied victory," warned Churchill. "From Stettin in the Baltic to Trieste in the Adriatic, an 'Iron Curtain' has descended across the continent. Behind that line lie all the capitals of the ancient states of Central and Eastern Europe.

"All these famous cities and the populations around them lie in what I must call the Soviet sphere, and all are subject in one form or another, not only to Soviet influence, but to a very high, and, in many cases, increasing measure of control from Moscow.

"Police states are prevailing in nearly every case, and so far . . . there is no true democracy."

These were harsh words, but the leaders of the Free World listened. They knew that from that moment on, Churchill had established a popular stand against Communism for everyone to follow.

For the next few years, Churchill's rival Labour Party remained in power at home. But its control deteriorated with the 1950 elections, when it held a slim 315–297 edge over the Conservatives in the House of Commons. Liberals maintained nine other seats, but the margin did not last long.

In the fall elections of 1951, the Labour Party polled 231,000 more popular votes than the Conservatives, but lost twenty seats. Once more, Winston Churchill took command, still powerful despite his advanced years. He was seventy-seven.

The first of Montgomery's predictions had come true. The second soon followed. In 1953, Queen Elizabeth II honored the statesman by elevating him to knighthood.

3

A Vision of Dealey Plaza

ERNESTO MONTGOMERY WAS A HIGHLY REGARDED CORPO-
ral in the Psychic Intelligence Division of the Jamaica Police
Department in 1957 and just beginning to rise through the ranks,
when he took a three-month study leave to come to Dallas,
Texas, and observe American crime-fighting techniques.

Skilled in fingerprint, ballistics and typewriter identification,
he carried with him a letter of recommendation from his own
chief, Commissioner of Police Colonel Reginold Mitchelin, to
Dallas Police Chief Jess Curry. But his brief sojourn in the United
States almost turned into a nightmare his first day.

Hungry, the frail policeman walked into a restaurant and sat
down. Moments later, a waitress brought him a menu and left it
for him to study.

One hour later, having scrutinized the printed words so
carefully that he might have been able to get a good make on
the printer, Montgomery was still waiting for the waitress to return.

Frustrated, his stomach growling and being stared at by
other patrons, he finally beckoned her to him and began to place

his order. But before he could tell the woman the type of dressing he wanted on his salad, her manager was at the table, too.

"We don't serve nigrahs," he slurred, and ordered the black man to leave. Montgomery was stunned, but quickly recovered. He was adamant. He insisted, courteously as he could, on a meal. The restaurant employees left him sitting there, his order still not taken.

A few minutes later, the psychic remembers feeling the presence of "blue." He looked up to see two of the biggest police officers he had ever seen. They were looming over him.

"Why are you makin' trouble for these good people?" the bigger of the two demanded.

"I'm not making trouble, mon. I just want to eat."

The officers grabbed him by the arms and started to drag him to his feet.

"Wait, mon, wait!"

As quickly as he could, Montgomery tried to explain that he was in Dallas as a guest of the commissioner of police, that he was here from Jamaica on an education program, to study.

The burly patrolmen interrupted their efforts to remove him forcibly from the restaurant long enough for him to produce a letter.

This communication had come from Dallas Chief Curry. It related how delighted the chief and his force were that they would be welcoming him to examine and evaluate American law enforcement techniques. Little did the police official realize how closely the foreigner would examine them.

The officers released their grip and let the would-be troublemaker slide back into his chair. They walked away and began whispering to the manager. Moments later, they were back, telling Montgomery that he would be served.

Seconds after the policemen turned their backs and walked out the door, the psychic's problems began anew.

"Hey, buddy, I don't think you better eat here," said a man coming toward him from a neighboring table. His attitude was friendly, but his words were not. "They can do anything they want to to your food back in that kitchen, you know."

Montgomery got the message. The waitress returned and asked for his order.

"No, thank you," he said. "I changed my mind."

The next morning, a squad car arrived at his residence to transport him to police headquarters. Ironically, the driver was one of the abusive officers from the night before.

Despite that one brush with the 1950s American racial prejudice, Montgomery enjoyed his stay immensely, even though his hosts were skeptical about psychics and the occult in general.

During his brief stay in Texas, he kept in touch with friends back home through the mails. It was in late July that he wrote them about a vision he had seen the night before.

It was a terrible sight. A railroad disaster was about to occur in his native land. Filled with unruly youngsters and being driven by an engineer who appeared drunk, a train would speed around a bend, hurtle from the tracks and plunge into the deep valley below.

Montgomery watched, horrified as the cars piled upon one another. He saw broken or severed limbs everywhere and heard passengers' screams. It was an unnerving sight that had kept him awake most of the night.

Four weeks later, the prediction became reality.

On September 1, 1957, a passenger train was winding through a mountain pass in Jamaica, when it suddenly lurched from the rails and tumbled down the steep slope.

More than 175 people were killed and hundreds more injured, as the cars accordioned to the valley bottom. It was the worst transportation disaster in local history.

Ernesto Montgomery's sharply honed psychic powers could not have prevented the rail mishap, but they could have been used to save the life of President John F. Kennedy.

Days after making the railroad forecast to friends, the seer was talking with Captain Slaughter, the officer assigned to give him a full rundown of Dallas police operations, Patrolman Gerald Hill, two other policemen and a press photographer when he perceived new, disturbing vibrations.

"I remember saying that tragedy was going to strike Dallas, maybe in a couple of years," he recalls. "But at that instant, I

didn't know what exactly it would be. All I knew was that I had
to see the routes parades normally take.

"I asked the captain to show me, and he brought out a map.
Everything went smoothly when he showed me routes along
Commerce, Main and Elm streets. But as soon as his fingers
reached Dealey Plaza, I knew what was going to happen.

"I say: 'Stop right there! A President of the United States is
going to be shot right there!'

"Everybody had a big laugh on me—everybody but the photographer. He said to wait and took a picture, but nobody paid it
any mind. Captain Slaughter was pointing to Dealey Plaza, and
I was standing beside him. The photograph ran in a black-
oriented weekly newspaper. The photographer later gave me a
copy."

At the time, with Eisenhower still occupying the White
House, Montgomery was not sure who the slain President
would be.

Two years later, after coming back to the United States for
good, he had a pretty good suspicion. It began to formulate soon
after he received a telephone call from an aide to then Senator
Kennedy, the Democratic candidate for President. The aide had
learned about Montgomery's prediction and wanted to know if
he had any more information.

"He asked, half facetiously, if they should let the other
fellow [Richard Nixon] win," the psychic remembers. "But I
reiterated that I still didn't have a name. A short while later,
though, I was able to say definitely that it was Mr. Kennedy. I
mentioned it to Patrolman Hill."

On November 22, 1963, almost six years to the day that
Montgomery ended his study leave to rejoin the Jamaica Police
Department, the youthful President's *Air Force One* touched
down at Dallas' Love Field. He was going to deliver a speech at
the Trade Mart.

Kennedy was riding with his wife, the former Jacqueline
Bouvier, Texas Governor John Connally and his wife, Nellie, in
the open Lincoln limousine nicknamed "Lancer," when his mo-
torcade reached downtown Dallas.

Under a hot Texas sun, with onlookers lined ten deep along

both curbs, the two men were discussing the President's warm reception. Just as the car turned right from Elm Street in to Dealey Plaza, Mrs. Kennedy complained of the heat.

Moments later, the first report rang out. An experienced hunter, Connally recognized the sound as gunfire. His eyes flashed frantically to the crowd on the right, searching desperately for the assassin. All he saw was a sea of blank faces staring back in awe. They still did not know. There was no telltale puff of smoke.

The governor was just beginning to swing his body around to the left to check the President, when the second blast came. He never saw Kennedy, as a bullet ripped through his chest.

"My God, they're going to kill us all," he gasped, as he collapsed into his wife's lap and started to cry.[1] Connally was wrong. Only the President would die.

Swaying a foot or two above the prone governor, Kennedy was dazed, too. His hand was at his neck, where the first bullet had struck. He remained standing only moments longer.

When the third blast followed, speeding a bullet on a fatal trajectory from the Texas School Book Depository building only a few yards across the way, the President's head exploded, splattering blood and brain tissue on the motorcycle patrolman following behind the car.

"God! They've killed my husband," his wife wailed. "His brains are on my hands."[2]

In a few seconds, it was over. But reverberations from that black noon hour in Dallas still are being felt. Kennedy was dead, and Lee Harvey Oswald was branded as the killer. In a few days, he, too, would no longer be alive.

The death car rolled to a halt at the exact site on the plaza where Ernesto Montgomery had said a presidential assassination would occur, the same location he had pointed to on the police map six years before. But those who had heard his dire warning only had laughed.

They laughed, just as too many authorities in responsible places are still laughing today at students of the assassination, investigators and psychics who insist that Oswald did not act alone.

Through soul travel and meditation, Dr. Montgomery learned that Oswald was only one of three armed assassins stationed in the vicinity of Dealey Plaza when the President was slain. Ironically, Oswald was the only one of the three who did not fire one of the two shots which struck Kennedy.

One of the conspirators was on a grassy knoll near the Book Depository and fired the second and fatal shot, the psychic learned when he traveled the soul plane back to the time of the slaying. The other shot was fired from the Book Depository, not by Oswald, but by his companion.

Oswald's co-conspirators escaped in a helicopter, which was standing by on a nearby building. Many people saw the helicopter but believed it to be owned by or on lease to a Dallas newspaper. It took off so fast that Oswald was left behind.

Dr. Montgomery learned that both men who escaped were later murdered, as were most of the lower echelon conspirators. Other assassinations of conspirators still alive will be carried out to insure silence as public demands for more information mount.

Meditation and trance disclosed that the conspiracy was Communist-backed and included Soviets, Red Chinese, Cubans and several powerful American political and governmental officials. The Red Chinese collaborated with the Russians, despite their ideological differences, because of their mutual conviction that Kennedy's strong, popular leadership was a threat to Communist world expansion.

"The Bay of Pigs invasion, even though it was a debacle, demonstrated to the Chinese that Kennedy would use force to maintain America's influence in the world. The Communists were determined that he had to die."

The Secret Service, FBI and other American investigative agencies know the truth about the assassination, Dr. Montgomery says, but it will be years before the true story is disclosed to the American public.

When the truth is known, former New Orleans District Attorney Jim Garrison will also be vindicated. "Mr. Garrison was on the right track when he opened his own investigation into the conspiracy, but he was destroyed for it."

Dallas police officials did not regard Montgomery's psychic

powers seriously during his brief 1957 stay, nor apparently did they do so with any other seer they might have encountered. But the Texan officials and the American life-style made a decidedly favorable impression on the visitor from the Caribbean.

From the moment he climbed aboard his airplane for Jamaica and home, Montgomery wanted to return.

"In Jamaica, I was only a little corporal. But I was on the way up," he recalled. "I was a guard commander, and I had responsibility. I had to train recruits in the functions of a police officer. I had to make them effective through drill and classes.

"It was nothing like the United States, where officers are on the force after only six months of training. In Jamaica, you are schooled eighteen months before going into the street. And then, you're on probation for two years before becoming a full-fledged cop."

Dr. Montgomery would probably be a deputy commissioner or superintendent of police today if he had remained in Jamaica. He was being considered for a new position, to be created especially as a result of his training in the United States.

In those days, most of the ranking police officers were white, and black Jamaicans were about to begin moving into the higher echelons of the department. As the only officer with training in the United States, Montgomery was slated for more responsibility and higher rank.

"But I was so impressed with the United States and with American police technology that I gave it all up," he says. "I believed that the opportunity for me as a police officer was in this country."

The Jamaican policeman, despite his unpleasant experience in the Dallas restaurant, was not aware of just how deep and widespread racism was in the United States, at that time. Even though many of the higher positions in government and in the police department in Jamaica were still held by whites, racism was not as obvious in other areas of daily Jamaican life.

"And the United States just looked so good that I saw only what I wanted to," he says. "To a foreigner, this country still gives the impression that the streets are lined with gold and dollars drip from every employment agency.

"People believe that you can just walk into a place and get a job that pays two or three hundred dollars a week. And they think that you only have to work for maybe half an hour a day, because most Americans are soft, potbellied and enjoy an easy life. It looked so easy.

"In Jamaica, too, we are so trim and in shape. So when I got here and saw the police driving around in cars, etc., I was amazed. We didn't drive around in cars; we walked a beat and stood for eight hours in the street."

So Montgomery resigned from his Psychic Intelligence Division post, putting out of his mind any advancement that had been in his future.

4

Dr. Montgomery Meets the Stars

ERROL FLYNN DID NOT LISTEN. NEITHER DID MARILYN Monroe. Nor Martin Luther King. Perhaps, if they had, some or all of them might be alive today. After all, Ernesto Montgomery gave each a fair warning.

Flynn blew into Jamaica in 1954. He loved the West Indies. He loved the countryside, the customs and the climate. He and his father, Professor Theodore Flynn, were considering purchase of Navy Island, a small outcropping of land near Port Antonio. They wanted to build a home there, a tropical retreat.

The actor was also thinking about filming the story of the infamous Miss Annie Palmer, the "White Witch of Rose Hall." Annie Palmer acquired her shameful sobriquet as a woman who took slave lovers and then killed them. She was finally killed herself, with a stake driven through her heart.

Flynn sailed to the Caribbean aboard the yacht *Zacca*, anchoring first at Port Antonio and then at Montego Bay before heading to Kingston. Along the way, he introduced water-skiing to Jamaica. He was a cocksure, brash, hard-drinking, quick-fisted man, much like the swashbuckling hero he was typecast as in films.

Born June 20, 1909, on Tasmania, south of Australia, Flynn was the son of a distinguished marine biologist, who was away most of the time, and an overbearing sea captain's daughter, who beat him often for minor childish indiscretions.

Love for the sea was in his blood. Pirate tales told by his grandfather heightened his interest. By the time he was seven, he and his mother were fighting constantly, and he ran away from home for the first time.

He slept on the beach for two nights, dining on plentiful island fruits, before visiting a local farmer and asking for work. The farmer obliged, giving him room, board and a few cents change for his labor. But he also contacted Flynn's father and sent the boy back home.

Flynn was bored with school. He played hooky often. Trouble dogged him. By age seventeen, he had been expelled from most of the best prep schools in Australia and Great Britain.

At the same time, he was engaged to marry Naomi Dibbs, one of the most eligible women from one of the wealthiest Tasmanian families. But when she gave him a choice of buckling down to his studies or ending their relationship, he ran all the way to New Guinea.

For the next seven years, Flynn worked as a ship's captain, plantation manager, soldier and con man. He polished his skills as a lover and often found himself in jail for committing adultery with other men's wives.

His entry into show business began in New Guinea, where he guided a film director into the back country to film several background scenes. The director was impressed by his guide and told him he wanted to use him in a movie some day. Flynn laughed.

Two years later, almost like something out of a film script itself, the call from Hollywood came. The director cast Flynn as Fletcher Christian in *In the Wake of the Bounty*. But one film, even though he enjoyed the work, was not enough to win him over. He returned to the South Pacific after the last scene was complete.

Two years later, stone broke, he made his way to England to begin an acting career once more, and eventually he joined the Northhampton Repertory Company. By 1935, a Warner Brothers talent scout attended a performance and was interested enough to sign Flynn to a six-month, $150-a-week contract. An additional clause provided the actor with a new wardrobe.

Several minor roles, including that of a corpse, followed before he starred in *Captain Blood,* with Olivia deHavilland. About the same time he began a love affair with Lili Damita, an established star and hot-tempered Latin. They eloped at the suggestion of a friend. It cost Flynn two dollars for the license—and more than a million dollars in alimony payments.

Two other marriages and other love affairs followed, interspersed with time out to volunteer in the Spanish Civil War. Yet he was bored. Flynn began smoking opium, emerged as one of the first known pot smokers in Hollywood and earned a reputation as one of the most dedicated drinkers in the film colony.

Troubles and alimony payments piled up. After an unsuccessful venture in Italy, where he plunged deeply in debt in an attempt to launch his own film company, Flynn turned his sights toward Jamaica. It was there that he met Dr. Montgomery.

"He was living a very, very fast life, and he came to me at the Central Police Station for a consultation one afternoon," the psychic recalled. "His visit took me by surprise. I told him he was living at too fast a pace and that he had to slow down. But this is what he said:

" 'Officer, I go to church, and I pay my tithe, and I am a God-fearing man. But life is worth living to the hilt.' He would not slow down, but would continue as he had in the past.

" 'Well, sir,' I said, 'if you fail to slow down, you're going to die, not tragically, but suddenly. A man in his forties, nightclubbing every night with young girls, sooner or later that behavior is going to catch up with you, and you will be no more.'

" 'Well,' Flynn replied, grinning as he rejected the warning, 'it's the good life.' "

Even though he did not accept Montgomery's reading and counsel, Flynn wanted to pay the young policeman for his services. As a member of the Psychic Division of the department, however, the seer could not accept.

Flynn offered the young policeman $500 for the consultation. When the money was refused, the actor said he would donate it to the *Jamaica Police Magazine*. Montgomery never learned if the actor carried through on the promise.

A few months after the meeting with Officer Montgomery, Flynn began accepting movie roles once more. He was typecast again. This time as a drunkard. By the time his third wife left him in 1958, his hard living and ruinous life-style were catching up with him, just as the seer had predicted.

Errol Flynn was lounging at the side of a swimming pool with his latest female companion, teen-ager Beverly Aadland, on October 14, 1959, when he collapsed and died of a heart attack. The man who had thrilled movie audiences outdueling hundreds of pirates and other assorted blackguards on the screen had also fought grim but more private battles with malaria, gonorrhea, tuberculosis, hepatitis, kidney and liver diseases. All by the time he was fifty.

Montgomery's encounter with Marilyn Monroe occurred a few months after the actress left the island in 1954. She had come there with her husband, Joe DiMaggio, in an attempt to save a failing marriage.

Already an established star, she had angered her husband on their honeymoon in Japan, when she agreed to leave him to appear briefly with the USO before American troops in Korea. It was good public relations for Marilyn as an actress, but a poor performance as a wife and got the marriage off to a rocky start.

When Dr. Montgomery talked to the actress at the Jamaica Central Police Station she was very poorly disguised in a red dress with a red turban covering her blond hair. A piece of the turban was pulled across one cheek. Her eyes were hidden behind dark glasses.

One of the topics they discussed was the "paranormal." At the time, it was not fashionable to discuss the "psychic world."

"She had done a lot of reading on the subject and was interested in yoga, psychism, soul travel and interpretation of dreams. She was an avid reader, and most of her information came from this. But she did make some mistakes. Her information was not flawless," Montgomery remembered.

Then, as now, the young policeman-psychic did not with-
hold any information that he perceived when counseling people.

"I presumed that if she came to see me, in all fairness I had
to tell her everything, for whatever it was worth. If I see an accident ahead, it is to the client's advantage that I tell them, because this gives him or her a chance to attempt to alter things by
using free will."

Free will, the psychic insists, can change many events slated
in a person's future by permitting them to avoid unpleasantness
through alternative action. "If a plane is going to fall, you can
tell the pilot not to fly that day. Obviously, then, the crash will
not occur."

Montgomery told the actress that she would be dead within
six years. As her eyes widened in shock, the psychic added that
she would die at the hands of someone else, but that her death
would be made to look like an accident.

His prediction was off by two years. Marilyn Monroe was
found in her bedroom on August 5, 1962, dead of an overdose of
barbiturates. Her death alternately was reported to be a suicide
and an accident. But some admirers of the late actress believe, as
Dr. Montgomery predicted, that she was murdered.

Some of the theories, admittedly, are bizarre. But books
have been written, theorizing that she was murdered by either
the CIA, the Communist Party or by self-styled protectors of the
late President John F. Kennedy and of his late brother, Senator
Robert F. Kennedy. Rumors have linked the beautiful actress to
both men.

As Montgomery talked, the color drained from Marilyn's
face. She was bewildered and frightened. She wanted to continue with the interview, but asked that the psychic concentrate
on her career instead of pursuing his premonition of her un-
timely death.

The outlook for her career also indicated a bumpy road
ahead. "You are going to have difficulties with one of your
movies. Not immediately, but there will be a movie that you will
have considerable trouble with. You will be fired and then
rehired," the psychic advised.

The interview ended with the actress thanking the clairvoyant for his advice and promising to be cautious. "But she said she thought I must have been picking up impressions from someone else, perhaps someone near to her, when I was talking about her death.

"Lots of people feel psychics are not 100 per cent correct, of course. So she wanted to believe that I was wrong. She tried to put it out of her mind."

By 1962, with a tragic childhood and three unhappy marriages behind her, Marilyn was seeing a psychiatrist regularly because of depression. She was taking barbiturates for her nerves and to sleep at night.

She had built a reputation of unreliability on the set, and it was getting her into serious trouble. On April 23, she began work on *Something's Got to Give*, a remake of *My Favorite Wife*, the 1939 Cary Grant classic.

But Marilyn was suffering from a viral infection she had caught in Mexico a short while before. Running a high fever, she tried to work, but could not. By early May, the 20th Century-Fox company had shot all it could without her.

"On Monday, May 14, the studio was ready to use Kim Novak or Shirley MacLaine as a replacement if Marilyn didn't show up that morning," reported Eunice Murray, Marilyn's companion, in *Marilyn: The Last Months*. "Marilyn showed up. She did a scene that day with two children, working the following day with Dean Martin.

"By Friday afternoon, however, she checked out to fly East for the President's [John F. Kennedy] Birthday Ball, set for May 19 at Madison Square Garden. The studio was irate. . . ."[1]

Nine days after the ball, Marilyn filmed her first nude scene ever, and the virus set in again. Three days later, she was out of a job. The studio halted production. Another two months, and she was dead of a drug overdose.

Only a few days before her death, Marilyn received word from 20th Century-Fox executives that they were planning to resume work on *Something's Got to Give*. She would still be in the starring role. Intimates remembered that she was pleased with the news.

Ernesto Montgomery may have missed her death by two

years, but he scored a direct hit when he said that it would be controversial. Although a coroner's jury ruled that she died of an "accidental" drug overdose, stories immediately began to surface, hinting of a darker, more ominous fate. Most of the rumors told or hinted at fatal love affairs with either President Kennedy or his brother Robert.

"They said she died of an overdose of sleeping pills. But I have looked into her life very carefully both before and after her death," said Montgomery. "There is no doubt: Marilyn Monroe was murdered. There are two celebrities who had something to do with it."

Montgomery agrees that an overdose of drugs was the direct cause of death, but he insists that the barbiturates were not taken willingly. "It is tragic. She might have changed her fate if she had listened to my advice."

Dr. Martin Luther King is another whose life might have been saved, had he heeded the Jamaican psychic's advice.

Dr. Montgomery was living in Hollywood and had established offices in south central Los Angeles, when the black leader visited local officials of the Southern Christian Leadership Conference a few months before his assassination.

One day, after telephoning, Dr. King walked into the psychic's office with two women and a male companion. The SCLC leader introduced himself, explained that he had heard of Dr. Montgomery's work as a psychic and as a Christian minister and said he was taking advantage of a break in his schedule for a meeting. At Dr. King's suggestion, Montgomery slipped into a preliminary trance state and began a reading.

When Dr. Montgomery has gone into preliminary trance, the alert observer can notice slightly slurred speech. Usually the psychic will appear to be dabbling with an area just above his ears, near his hairline.

The "dabbling" has a purpose. It is usually an indication that he is activating his antennae, a process that he resorts to only occasionally because their sensitivity makes them painful to touch.

On this particular occasion, however, because of Dr. King's limited time and because of the effectiveness of the method,

Montgomery used his antennae. He saw muddy water, a sign of death. There was also a voice, but it was too faint to determine the message.

The psychic told Dr. King that his life was in grave jeopardy. He advised the civil rights leader that an attempt would definitely be made on his life and urged him to be especially security conscious during the next several months.

"He wasn't at all upset. He didn't even raise an eyebrow," Montgomery remembers. "He was very nonchalant about it and took the attitude that what will be, will be. He was a brave man, with a tremendous amount of pride."

A few months later, in late March 1968, Montgomery was meditating about Dr. King when he again saw a vision of muddy water. It was churning and turbulent. The meaning was clear enough. Heavyhearted and with the uneasy premonition that the Nobel Peace Prize winner's fate was already sealed, Montgomery wrote him a letter that night. He reminded Dr. King of the previous warning, told him of the new vision and cautioned that the danger was imminent.

On April 4, 1968, Dr. King was shot to death on the balcony of a Memphis hotel by assassin James Earl Ray.

Montgomery believes that Dr. King never read the letter. "As you know, thousands of letters were written to him every day, and I'm afraid that my warning was thrown away or was still waiting unopened when he died. That's why in my work today, I tell everyone that no matter what comes in the mail, it must be read. A letter, no matter how innocent it may appear to be at first glance, can be of significance."

One person who has listened to Montgomery's counsel with positive results is Dorrie Dixon, a huge, heavily muscled man, who won the 1952 Mr. Jamaica Body Beautiful Contest. Dixon studied for a time to be a minister, but, instead, became a bodyguard for a Mexican government official and later a professional wrestler.

Montgomery first met Dixon at Montego Bay, the wrestler's birthplace, but their paths have crossed many times since, both in Jamaica and in various cities in the United States. By the time they met in Los Angeles in 1972, Dixon was internationally known for his skill on the mat, and Montgomery was building a reputation of his own as a psychic and cleric.

Looking into his friend's future, Montgomery foresaw a financially successful tour of the West Coast. That was not too surprising, because Dixon was a top-ranked wrestler and was especially popular with black fans.

More startling was the psychic's prediction that before Dixon's contracted tour of West Coast cities was completed, he would be offered a movie role.

Dixon had already appeared in several movies filmed in Mexico, but was not anticipating any film offers from Hollywood. Two weeks after his conference with Montgomery, Dixon was telephoned by a Hollywood film executive and asked to come to the studios. The executive said he had watched Dixon on television, was impressed by his physique and had a part for him in a movie, *Melinda*. The movie starred Calvin Lockhart, Vonetta McGee, Rosalind Cash, and Earl Maynard, another friend of Dr. Montgomery's.

Dixon was also advised that his wrestling career would extend until 1981, when he will retire in financial security.

Dr. Montgomery added advice about Dixon's family, urging him to invest in Jamaican real estate. Dixon was planning to make real estate investments in Mexico, which Montgomery told him were safe. "But I also urged him to invest in Jamaican real estate, because he will return in later life and domicile permanently there."

Dixon has listened to Dr. Montgomery, and has prospered. The Los Angeles Police Department has also listened to the psychic at times and profited.

With Dr. Montgomery's assistance, Los Angeles police helped avert an assassination attempt against comedian Bob Hope. If they and other law enforcement agencies had listened to more of his warnings, the Sharon Tate murders, the slaying of Robert F. Kennedy and much of the Symbionese Liberation Army terrorism might also have been avoided.

5

A Warning Heeded;
Warnings Ignored

COMEDIAN BOB HOPE ALWAYS HAS DONE HIS UTMOST TO bring quality entertainment to American troops stationed overseas, whether in peacetime Europe, war-torn Korea or Southeast Asia.

But he was far from combat zones and enemy bullets in 1970, when Dr. Ernesto Montgomery's psychic warning of an assassination attempt apparently saved his life.

On February 28, the Jamaican seer entered into soul travel to gather specific information about Hope's life. Immediately, he saw muddy waters moving to surround the entertainer. A violent death was imminent.

"It was during the anti-war demonstrations," Montgomery says. "I was concerned with Mr. Hope's involvement in the war as a morale booster."

The psychic saw the comedian seated in his home late at night, reading a newspaper and drinking a cup of coffee. Suddenly, a gun appeared at the window. A long-haired assassin squeezed the trigger, and a bullet crashed into Hope's skull. The force of the impact hurled the entertainer backward against the chair. Then he slumped forward and sprawled on the floor, dead.

Alarmed, Montgomery called a hurried press conference and police briefing for March 2. He immediately dispatched warnings to all local radio and television outlets, to area police departments and to the mayor of Los Angeles.

He had called briefing sessions in his Los Angeles office (it was later moved to Hollywood) in the past to announce major predictions of events clairvoyantly observed. They were sparsely attended, if at all. Coming on the heels of a futile warning of a gruesome massacre only a few months earlier, however, his admonition drew serious attention from both police and the press this time.

Detectives D. B. Crist and N. E. Eggert from the Los Angeles County Sheriff's Department, Sergeant Daniel Cook with the LAPD, Gene Sheppard, a reporter with NBC news, and several others attended the press conference.

They listened intently as Montgomery revealed that members of an "anti-Vietnam committee" were conspiring to murder Hope to gain attention to their cause and to eliminate one of the most visible supporters of American leaders in the White House and the Pentagon. The group of left-wing radicals was opposed to all involvement in Southeast Asia.

"They believe that if they can kill Mr. Hope, who is so involved in the American cause, that they will shock and disturb the American people so much that everyone will demand immediate withdrawal from combat," he told assembled police and reporters.

"Of course, acting under what they believed to be proper methods of true idealism, they were wrong. Instead of winning sympathy, they only would have hindered their cause. They might even have forced the actual pullout to be delayed longer than it was."

Hope had angered anti-Vietnam radicals with his spirited support of the war effort and his calls for stronger action to defeat the Communists and bring the conflict to a close.

Although the GIs appreciated Hope's annual entertainment tours, as their fathers had, he ran into trouble with dissident elements on the home front when he talked of maintaining the free-

dom of the Vietnamese and warned that protests and demonstrations were helping the enemy.

Asked once by a reporter about his "aggressiveness" in sup-
porting the action in Vietnam he conceded that he would
"rather be a hawk than a pigeon." He incurred further wrath
from anti-war factions when he openly pressed his friendship
with President Nixon and Vice President Agnew, both seen as
villains of the war tableau.

In 1971 the New York City Council of Churches, yielding to
pressure from a group of young activist clergymen, canceled its
plans to present Hope with its 1971 Family of Man Award, because he had "uncritically supported the military establishment"
and the war in Vietnam.

Hope's reaction? "I appreciate the Americans who have laid
down their lives for our country. I got hooked on that thing, and
if that stops me from getting awards, then I'll have to live with
it."

But portents of more ominous reactions to Hope's dogged
determination to support the troops in Southeast Asia and the
Administration in Washington were developing.

Montgomery's audience listened soberly as he described
how radicals would strike at Hope, whom they saw as a hated
symbol of American determination in Vietnam. The assassination would be carried out on April 18, slightly more than two
weeks away, Montgomery said. Interest rose as he described the
killer.

Police beefed up protection of the comedian, and the band
of assassins apparently were scared off. The warning had successfully frustrated the planned attempt against his life.

A warning voice from Montgomery may have also pre-
vented a murder attempt on the life of Massachusetts Senator
Edward M. Kennedy, at the Democratic National Convention in
Chicago two years earlier.

On July 23, 1968, the clairvoyant alerted agent Joe Davis of
the Los Angeles FBI office and A. E. Sherman of the Secret Service that Kennedy would be an assassination target if he attended
the convention. When the convention opened a few weeks later,
Senator Kennedy was not there, although he had been expected

to attend. He stayed away as Democrats selected Hubert H. Humphrey as their presidential candidate.

The streets of Chicago were red with the blood of anti-Vietnam demonstrators before the convention was concluded. Radical youths clashed with police as violence raged outside the Chicago Amphitheater and on the streets north to the Loop. Among weapons seized by police were three high-powered rifles equipped with sniperscopes. They were similar to the rifle recovered from the Book Depository after President Kennedy's assassination in Dallas in 1963.

Montgomery, it appears, was instrumental in preventing Edward Kennedy's attendance at the riot-torn convention and thus probably saved his life. He was not so fortunate when it came to Edward's brother, Robert, a few months earlier.

Only a few weeks before the California presidential primary in 1968, the psychic envisioned RFK being swept away by muddy waters. Death was waiting for him.

"I tried to warn the police department three or four weeks before Mr. Kennedy was killed. I sent letters to Mayor Samuel Yorty, the city council, and the police chief to warn them about what was going to happen. That time, though, I got no response. They ignored me."

Kennedy was celebrating a solid political victory at the Ambassador Hotel in Los Angeles on the night of June 5, 1968, when Sirhan B. Sirhan lurched at him, elbowed the crowd away and gunned him down.

Seven years later on an assignment for *The National Tattler*, Montgomery visited the shooting scene in the kitchen of the hotel, in an attempt to divine if the Arab assassin was working alone. Using psychometry, picking up psychic vibrations from the surroundings, he concluded:

"Public pressure is going to be such that it will force officials to reopen the case within six months." The investigation was reopened less than six months later. Once again his psychic insight was proven correct.

Dr. Montgomery said there were two other Arab members of the assassination team in the area when RFK was slain. One was a man, the other a woman. The psychic saw them as instruments in a complex long-term conspiracy devised by Americans. Dr. Martin Luther King, he says, was another of their victims.

Robert Kennedy died because of his opposition to the war in Vietnam and because of his support for the Israelis in the Middle East, says Montgomery. Although new evidence will be uncovered in the renewed investigation, it will not be disclosed and the major conspirators never will be brought to trial.

Almost a year to the day after Senator Kennedy was slain, Montgomery received his first psychic warnings of the impending deaths of several prominent people in Hollywood.

The psychic was seated at his desk in a self-imposed light trance on June 16, 1969, when the warning vision took shape. Sweat bathed his forehead as terrible images formed in a chilling tableau. He saw the brutal, bloody murders of five men and women. The massacre would occur on or about August 9.

"I could see the people in my vision, but I didn't know who they were or exactly where they were at. All I knew was that it was somewhere in Benedict Canyon. I didn't pick up the exact address of the house."

Dr. Montgomery could see the killers clearly enough to determine that they were young men and women. Other features were too vague to make out.

That same day, the Jamaican-born seer wrote letters to several film stars who lived in the area. They included Dana Andrews, Gene Autry, Tony Curtis and Joan Fontaine. Each letter read:

> I am endowed with the gift of prophecy. I have had thousands of correct predictions to my credit, the difficult and most agonizing moment of my life is to be unable to warn someone of impending disaster or danger.
>
> Relative to my psychic vision, five prominent persons will be murdered on or about the 9th of August 1969 on Cielo Dr. in Benedict Canyon. I do not remember the correct digit of the address. I think it is 10060 or 10005 however if a warning could be given to the inhabitants of the entire area of the impending disaster the tragedy will be averted.
>
> I have had unpleasant experiences with the officials of Los Angeles County in trying to warn of other tragedies that

could be avoided. I cannot afford the television, radio or newspaper advertisement required that would be effective. I am resolute in my conviction that you will take the necessary step in warning the entire area on my behalf.

Miss Wanda Sue Parrot of the Los Angeles Herald Examiner and Mr. James J. McGuinn, director of Print Public Relations Intercommunication of Los Angeles can vouch as to many already fulfilled and interesting predictions.

Please find enclosed for your information a fact sheet. Wishing you all the best.

> Sincerely yours,
> Dr. Ernesto A. Montgomery:
> Prophet.

Recalling past frustrations with local police, the psychic believed letters to possible victims might bring about the best result. He was wrong. Each letter came back unopened.

"And for some reason, all of the addresses had been scratched out by someone. I realize now that my envelopes could have been mistaken for an appeal for a donation or for some other business reason, and the person to whom they were addressed simply didn't bother to open them.

"And due to the famous people living in the vicinity where I thought the murders would take place, there was no possibility of calling them by telephone. All such numbers are unlisted, you know.

"A letter was the only way."

Among those who never received the important message were film producer Roman Polanski and his beautiful, pregnant wife, actress Sharon Tate, who had achieved recent stardom in *Valley of the Dolls*. They lived at 100050 Cielo Drive. He was in London on August 8, while she was entertaining at home.

Jay Sebring, the popular men's hair stylist and Miss Tate's former fiancé, was there. Even though she had broken their engagement to marry Polanski, he and the director had become close friends.

Also present was Voityck Frokowsky, Polanski's childhood friend, whose family had financed some of the director's first films in their native Poland.

Abigail Folger, heiress to the Folger coffee fortune had accompanied him to the Polanskis' for the night. They dated steadily. It was a fatal mistake.

Steven Parent made the same error. He was on the mansion grounds, visiting caretaker William Garretson. It would be his last visit with anyone.

A maid, Mrs. Winifred Chapman, was lucky; she lived elsewhere. When she reported for work on August 9, the carefully manicured grounds surrounding the handsome Tate house looked like a battlefield. Two bodies were sprawled grotesquely on the lawn. Young Parent was slumped at the wheel of his car.

She screamed and ran. She was hysterical but managed to gasp out news of her grisly find to a neighborhood youth. He telephoned police. It took officers only a few minutes to substantiate Mrs. Chapman's story.

The first body was in the drive, where Parent, eighteen, was slumped behind the wheel of his Rambler automobile, shot five times. Nearby, on the front lawn, police found the body of Frokowsky, thirty-seven, stabbed and shot.

A few yards away the butchered body of his girl friend, Abigail Folger, was curled around the base of a fir tree. She was clad only in a nightgown.

Signs of the bloodbath were scattered throughout the house. But it was in the living room that the killers had left the most appalling remains of their ghastly handiwork. It was there that officers found Miss Tate and Sebring. Their bodies were linked with a common nylon rope, which had been looped over a rafter. Clad in a see-through nightgown and maternity bra, she had been slashed and stabbed repeatedly. Sebring had been stabbed and shot.

The carnage stopped short of the nearby guesthouse, where Garretson was found asleep. He was immediately arrested. Two days later he was cleared of complicity in the mass murder and released from custody. Eventually, he sued police for false arrest.

As Ernesto Montgomery had predicted, five people were murdered on Cielo Drive in Benedict Canyon "on or about the 9th of August."

But the killings did not stop at the Tate mansion. One day

later, with stories of the massacre on Cielo Drive dominating news in the nation's print and electronic media, Leno LaBianca, forty-four, owner of a supermarket chain, and his wife, Rosemary, thirty-eight, returned to their handsome home in the Los Feliz district of midtown Los Angeles from a day of water-skiing. They were never seen alive again.

Frank Struthers, fourteen, Mrs. LaBianca's son by a previous marriage, with a friend, discovered the bodies the next morning.

His stepfather was in the living room, his body shredded with stab wounds. The word "war" was carved on his chest. A pillowcase covered his head. A fork had been plunged into his stomach.

His mother was in the bedroom, hacked to death.

At the murder sites, the killers had written the messages "Political Piggies" and "Death to Pigs" in the victims' blood.

For weeks after the bodies were found, Montgomery suffered terribly.

"I had an awful feeling of depression," he recalls. "To think that I am cursed with this ability and still am not able to prevent such things from happening."

As he recovered, however, he offered his special services to officials of Los Angeles County in an effort to solve the crimes. Again, he was refused.

Finally, on October 3, 1969, the psychic entered trance to learn what he could.

"I saw the name 'Charlie' in my mind and then the name 'Mansoon.' I knew then that this man was leader of the group responsible for the killings."

Immediately, Montgomery supplied the information to the Los Angeles City News Service, United Press International, the Los Angeles *Times,* the Los Angeles *Citizens News,* the San Francisco *Chronicle,* radio station KFWB, the Folger's Coffee Company, the mayor, police chief, local district attorney and to friends of Roman Polanski.

One month later, on November 6, when he lectured at California State College-Los Angeles, he predicted that the case would be solved by the end of the year.

During the week ending December 1, police announced a break in the investigation and the arrest of several people, including Charles Manson, the bearded, wild-eyed leader of a drug and sex cult.

Charged with him were Patricia Krenwinkel, twenty-one, Leslie Van Houten, nineteen, Linda Louise Kasabian, twenty, Charles "Tex" Watson, twenty-four, and Susan Denise Atkins, twenty-one.

Manson was convicted and imprisoned with others of his tribe. But he and his followers did not drop out of the news with his imprisonment. In early 1975 Manson was transferred from one California prison to another for his own protection after tangling with fellow convicts.

Then, on September 3, 1975, Dr. Montgomery had an unsettling vision of President Gerald Ford in trouble. He was being smothered by a blood-red haze. The psychic told friends that he was fearful there would be an attempt on the President's life. It would be soon, he said, no longer than a few weeks.

Two days later a tiny young woman wearing a scarlet robe with a hood that gave her the appearance of a Satanic elf, lunged at the President with a gun as he was walking through a crowd in Sacramento, California. The gun misfired, and she was quickly overpowered and disarmed by a host of Secret Servicemen. Lynette Alice "Squeaky" Fromme, twenty-six, had been Manson's lieutenant and had frequently bragged about her skill with firearms.

Sandra Good, "Squeaky's" red-robed roommate and another Manson girl, stated that the would-be assassin tried to shoot the President in a protest against firms that are polluting the environment.

"Squeaky" Fromme's assassination attempt of President Ford was frustrated. Today, years after the public first heard of Charles Manson and his followers, Montgomery still asks himself the question: "Could Sharon Tate and the others have been saved?"

The answer is always the same: "Yes. If my warning had only gotten through and been believed."

6

A Church Is Founded

A MAJOR PORTION OF DR. ERNESTO MONTGOMERY's work today deals with the Universal Metaphysical Church, a church without walls, which he founded in 1966.

It is dedicated to the philosophy of teaching men and women to enjoy the peace and harmony within themselves, to experience peace of mind and harmonious relationships.

Montgomery maintains business offices in Hollywood, but keeps no formal house of worship. Instead, he takes his ministry to the people in the form of lectures and healing services at auditoriums, halls, churches and other meeting places from coast to coast, and through the mails.

Monzel Wickliffe, a systems analyst for a West Coast planning, design, architecture and engineering firm, is Montgomery's right-hand man. Wickliffe, an energetic, enterprising individual, is Montgomery's idea man and behind-the-scenes organizer.

Whether the psychic appears at the Los Angeles Coliseum or launches a national lecture tour, the scheduling and arrangements are usually the responsibility of Wickliffe. Sometimes there is other volunteer help, but more often there is not.

The two men met after a girl friend of Wickliffe's one time

suggested, only half seriously, that he talk to a psychic. Wickliffe talked with one. A week later, he heard of Dr. Montgomery and talked with him.

"He told me some of the same things the other psychic had told me. I was impressed." The acquaintance rapidly blossomed into a friendship, then a business relationship. It's a valuable alliance for Dr. Montgomery. Wickliffe's expertise with the computer is beneficial in keeping current the 7,800-member membership lists of the church and in insuring that the business end of the enterprise runs smoothly.

Trained in the exactness of mathematics, computers and organizational structure, Wickliffe handles the business end of running a church without walls with equanimity.

It is Dr. Montgomery's amazing ability to see into the future that continues to shake him.

"His powers still give me an odd feeling, even after all this time together," Wickliffe admits. "I remember when he was consulting with a Los Angeles family and told the husband, who was unemployed, not to drive on a certain day. The guy drove anyway, and was killed in an accident.

"Dr. Montgomery was shaken by the death. I had been working with him from September to May, but I was awed. I've seen his work before, but I still can't get used to it. Sometimes it gives me the chills."

The two men have based their working relationship on a handshake. There are no contractual obligations on either side. "I just think Dr. Montgomery has a need, and I can do the job for him."

Wickliffe's work helps insure that each month members of the church, from as far away as Germany, the West Indies, Canada, Nigeria, Ethiopia, Ireland and Mexico receive inspirational letters, small Bibles, religious tracts and communications about Dr. Montgomery's Kingdom Plan.

The Kingdom Plan is the primary funding source for Dr. Montgomery's philanthropic ventures. It is through the monthly mailings to and from members of the Kingdom Plan that the Universal Metaphysical Church is held together.

The plan works for members in three areas of their lives: The mental, spiritual and physical.

There are seven basic steps to the plan, as outlined by Dr. Montgomery in cassette taped introductions he mails to new members:

1. Giving. "Give and it shall be given unto you" (LUKE 6:38).
2. Goal. "I have proposed it, I will also do it" (ISAIAH 46:11).
3. Visualization. "Where there is no vision, people perish" (PROVERBS 29:18).
4. Meditation. "In his law doth he meditate" (PSALMS 1:2).
5. Prayer. "The effectual fervent prayer of a righteous man availeth much" (JAMES 5:16).
6. Action. "Why sit here until we die?" (KINGS 7:3).
7. Praise. "Enter into His gates with thanksgiving and praise" (PSALMS 100:4).

The basic premise of the Kingdom Plan is that by giving, the participant is starting a cycle by which he will receive.

The concept of seed money is not new. It is tied to a natural law of the universe and to nature's system of replenishment. Plant a tiny seed, and under the proper conditions, it will grow and yield many times its original weight or value.

Planting seed money works similarly. Giving sets up a reaction in the superconscious, and money given with the knowledge and solid belief that it will be replenished, returns tenfold. The secrets of seed money and of helping oneself with one's own psychic powers are positive thinking, belief and prayer.

"Everything revolves in circles," Montgomery explains. "In your everyday activities, sometimes you yearn for the success that seems to be almost within your grasp, and somehow you are never able to reach it.

"The reason for this is that, instead of thinking positively and using your upper mind, negativism intrudes on your subconscious. You, too, can be successful if at this psychological moment you start to think positively and completely that you desire to manifest a certain factor in your personal life."

The psychic-minister instills the conviction in his church members that they are the most important people in the world.

He teaches that each individual is "heir to the Kingdom" and as such should consider himself to be a king.

"A king does not go through life cringing or feeling defeated," he says. "He doesn't go through life begging, but he commands and controls the forces of life and wins the hearts of his subjects.

"With the magnetic control of the Kingdom Plan, a person can find love, knowledge and the basic understanding to cope with everyday problems. If applied properly to his life, his life will be changed for the better."

It is important for the individual to build a new self-image and to proclaim that he is a son of God, heir to the universe.

"Do not forget the seven basic steps of the Kingdom Plan," Montgomery stresses. "These seven steps are of paramount importance. To move ahead, you must take them and apply them to your life accordingly.

"Giving opens the door to God's storehouse. When you give, it will give you the idea that you will be receiving tenfold. In due time, this idea manifests in your life and causes this thought to become a factor in your development.

"Give with an open heart, with the idea and understanding that you are giving to receive tenfold. The manifested fact of God's goodness will be of paramount importance, and you will receive tenfold.

"Goal is the next step. You have to decide what you want in this life. You must decide what you want. Once the decision is made and your sights are set to acquire that goal, then the goal will manifest.

"Visualization is very important," Montgomery says. "You must see in your mind the things that you want to accomplish. Visualization is the method in which you project a thought wave so that what you need may become a reality.

"This is a simple, basic tenet. When you set yourself and say to yourself: 'Well, I need a new car,' picture yourself sliding behind the wheel of a new automobile and driving. As you drive, picture yourself owning the car and everything necessary to purchase it.

"You may need a new home. All you have to do is picture

yourself living in a castle, in a mansion. As you picture yourself, visualize yourself living there. God's power will make this visualization a reality.

"But you have to put these laws into action to get them to work for you," he notes. "Visualization is one of the most important areas of the Kingdom Plan.

"If you are resolute in your conviction that you need a change in your life, visualization can make it so. When you visualize, you can visualize a divergence of things. It may not be a car or home, but it may be for your health or happiness.

"Think back to your childhood. Think of the happy life you lived years ago, and visualize that through God's power you are again living this happy life.

"Then through meditation, you will live the kind of life you visualize and that you need. Meditation relaxes the mind and spirit and increases the efficiency mentally and spiritually.

"Prayer comes next. Through prayer, you are able to verbalize your desires, making the impression stronger on your heart and moving God in your behalf."

Then the person must take action on his own, Montgomery says. "Go and do the thing you have been concentrating on. Do not put it off for another day. The change that you desire will come now.

"Then, do not forget praise. This is an important part of personal religious therapy. It brings God's blessing. Do not forget to praise God as soon as you receive all you asked for. Do not be ashamed to say: 'I thank you, Father, for the goodness You have done by causing this to be a factor in my life.' "

Does the Kingdom Plan work? Every day, Montgomery receives proof in the form of testimony from those lives that have been changed. Here are but a sample few of the thousands:

Dear Rev. Montgomery:
I am now relocated in Nashville with a new apartment and new work which I like better than my old job.
My health is better and I am finding peace now that I have the benefits of your wonderful Kingdom Plan. I no longer have the pains in my hips and back, and I'm sure

that my money troubles will be solved soon, with your continued blessings.

Your prayers have been with me and made everything that has happened to me possible.

R. A.
Nashville, Tennessee

Brother Montgomery:

Thank God I have been delivered by the Holy Spirit. Your ministry has helped me learn to walk in His path and avoid the traps of Satan. My life is improving daily since I have begun to read the Scriptures that you sent me, and to praise His name. My husband has come back home. I have stopped nagging him and he has a job. He hasn't been drinking for three weeks. Please continue to send your prayers to us. Praise be.

Mrs. K. D.
Hoboken, New Jersey

Dear Dr. Montgomery

I have all the work I want to do . . . and even at home I am always making some money. But the most important thing that happened was the woman who gave me the most trouble and worried me so much with my husband, is now a friend who always needs me. God brought her down so low, I even had to get up out of my bed to take her to work also lead [sic] her money. I can truly say I always want to keep the love of God in my heart and keep my life clean where I can serve God with a clean and pure heart. It's truly more than my husband can bear. He didn't think it could be done. Dr. Ernesto I thank God for you because so many things that is good has happened to me. . . .

Mrs. M. P.
Newton, Alabama

Dear Ernesto Montgomery:

I am so happy in my life since you started sending me your blessings for good health and happiness.

I have a good woman now who came to me after I received your cassettes and began living my life according to your Kingdom plan.

She has a good job, and I got a 50-cent raise (an hour) after using your visualization plan. I am also getting along better with my boss, and I have a new attitude about my work. I am continuing to pray, and do not forget to praise God for the blessings He has already sent me.

B. F. S.
Lubbock, Texas

Dear Dr. Montgomery:

Received your message about 12 days or so ago, when I was in very bad shape. I could not walk without my crutches. I followed your directions and feel much better. I am still kind of sore and stiff, but these last two or three days, I've felt better than I've felt in over a year. I really want to thank you for your prayers. I am praying, too. I have been trying to get disability for the last five years and haven't gotten anything yet. But I know with your prayers and mine, the Lord will open a way.

Mrs. M. C.
Hopkinsville, Kentucky

My dear, loving minister:

Holy greeting in the name of Jesus Christ. Dr. Montgomery, I am happy today that God is blessing me and my home in a great way. Last month, my husband became sick and had a deafness in both ears. But when I received your letter, that very same day, I noticed the change in his condition. Now he is normal again, thank God. Thank God for you and your great ministry.

Yes, I know that you are praying for me, because God is blessing my home and my body is being healed. I am living a new life and have more faith in God and the God in me. He is working miracles in my home and affairs. I am thanking God and you for the Kingdom Plan. It has given me a new lease on life, praise God.

I am enjoying the abundant life that Jesus came to bring to a dark world, and he sent you to deliver his peoples.

L. M. T.
Harrisburg, Pennsylvania

But Kingdom Plan members are not the only ones who benefit from the program. So, too, do children.

The Universal Metaphysical Church is helping support an orphanage in Tecate, Mexico, a few miles outside of Tijuana and the American border. Dr. Montgomery heard that conditions there were deplorable. The children, he was told, did not have enough to eat. There were not enough beds. They had hardly any clothing. There were not enough books in the school. He drove to Tecate to see for himself.

"When I saw how bad it was, I returned to San Diego and bought all the food I could get. Those children were going to bed hungry every night. The next time I went to Tecate, I loaded my car with bread before I started out."

The orphans of Tecate raise their own chickens, pigs and rabbits. One time, the orphanage acquired a shotgun, which was used to shoot wild rabbits for food. Mexican police took the gun away.

Time and already strained finances of the Universal Metaphysical Church have not permitted a concerted fund-raising drive to help the orphans. Assistance from Dr. Montgomery and the church has been sporadic, coming as funds are available. The need is growing faster than the means of assisting the children.

Other individuals and non-profit agencies help the orphan children of Tecate, but there is never enough. Many of the orphans, from six months to seven years old, suffer from scalp, skin and intestinal disorders. Some have had healings from Dr. Montgomery.

His humanitarian efforts are also familiar to the poor of Los Angeles, where he acquires and co-ordinates donations from toy companies and private donors during the Christmas holidays. Each Christmas he obtains names of needy families from the California Department of Public Social Services and distributes toys and food.

He is also founder and president of the Youth Opportunities League, working with poor children in Los Angeles. Here too, however, lack of sufficient funding has prevented launching of a large-scale assistance program.

"I'm concerned with poor children everywhere," Dr. Montgomery says. "But the church is concentrating its efforts on helping the children of Tecate. They are younger, and they are poorer. There are dozens of government and private agencies in the United States, to help children here. But those kids in Mexico aren't being supported by anyone."

7

A Day with a Psychic

IT WAS 10:30 A.M. AND THE CALIFORNIA SUN WAS HIGH overhead when Dr. Montgomery jockeyed his twelve-year-old white Cadillac into a parking place in the 5900 block of Melrose Avenue, Hollywood.

He climbed out of the car, adjusted his tie, pulled down the tail of his sport jacket, peeked at the white carnation in his buttonhole and strode purposefully inside the sprawling office building.

Two women, one black, the other Mexican-American, were already waiting in front of the entrance to his suite. He greeted them, opened the door and showed them to chairs in his downstairs office. A stack of magazines was arrayed on a table next to the chairs.

If the ladies would make themselves comfortable and wait, he would be with them as soon as possible.

Dr. Montgomery climbed the stairs to his second-floor offices. Then, dropping to his knees between a filing cabinet and a table filled with boxes of letters, he knelt before a simple cross on the wall and prayed.

Refreshed by his communion with the Creator, Dr. Montgomery arose after a few minutes, retraced his steps to the downstairs office and seated himself at his desk. There, he cupped his chin in the palms of his hands, extended his long fingers along the side of his face and closed his eyes in meditation.

Moments later he was ready to talk with his first client of the day.

She was an attractive woman, except for the swollen, discolored flesh around one eye. She was in her late twenties and had a trim figure, which was displayed well in a smart white pants suit that contrasted pleasantly with her smooth, dark skin. Dr. Montgomery had talked with her before. Several times.

Three months ago she had come to him, explaining that she heard about him from a friend whom he had counseled. Dr. Montgomery had helped the friend, and now, she said, she was hopeful he could help her. The problem wasn't an untypical one.

Married, she had several children and a husband with two jobs and one more woman than law or convention allowed. When the wife insisted that the other woman had to go, he moved in with his girl friend instead. The family was left without a husband and father and without financial support.

Dr. Montgomery advised the distraught wife to send the children to stay with relatives, file with county and state authorities for help in forcing the errant husband to pay child support and move to a new home. She should obtain a job for herself and begin a new life. Definitely do not give the husband either the new telephone number or address, he cautioned.

She followed the advice. The children went to the South to live with her mother until she could send for them. She got a job as a hostess in a nice Los Angeles restaurant and moved to a new apartment, obtaining a telephone with an unlisted number.

Her new life started to take shape. Without the daily round of fights and quarreling with her husband, she eased off the heavy drinking that had begun to intrude on her life, and her nerves settled down. She started to meet new friends.

Two weeks ago she had telephoned Dr. Montgomery to tell him about the job. If things kept going as they were, she said, she would be sending for her children soon. Dr. Montgomery advised her to wait for a while yet. She still needed some time to reorder her own life and to get her emotions under control before resuming the responsibility of mothering her children. The little ones were doing just fine with her mother, he reassured her.

Now she was confronting him with fire in her eye. "I did everything you said, and look what that man did to me," she accused, pointing to her swollen, discolored eye. Dr. Montgomery looked.

"Calm down," he soothed, raising his hands as she began to talk again. "Something is wrong here. Now, tell me exactly what happened, and we will find out what went wrong."

It wasn't easy for her to put the story in order. But with patient coaching from the clergyman, it finally began to take shape. Her husband had telephoned Georgia to talk to his children. His mother-in-law gave him his wife's new telephone number and address.

Under gentle prompting by Dr. Montgomery, the woman admitted she had agreed to a meeting when her husband telephoned. They quarreled immediately, but she eventually consented to send for the children and to give the marriage another try. The couple agreed to maintain their separate apartments until the children arrived at the airport, and then they would go home together to the wife's home.

The husband showed up at the airport with his girl friend to meet the children. It was an ill-conceived experiment.

The wife slapped the girl friend. The husband tried to separate the two women, and when his wife kicked him in the shins, he doubled his fist and hit her in the eye.

It didn't take long for Dr. Montgomery to help the woman realize that it was only after she had stopped following his instructions that her troubles resumed. While she was staying away from her husband, she was rebuilding her life and living a calm and reasonably happy existence. When she resumed her relationship with him, her troubles started over again. Immediately.

"Move again," he told her, "and this time tell your mother not to give your new address or your telephone number to your husband. You are going to have to accept a new life and make new friends. Go now, do what I told you to do, and I will pray for you."

Dr. Montgomery didn't call on his psychic powers to deal with the woman's problem. It wasn't necessary. As a Christian minister he has counseled hundreds of couples and individuals about domestic troubles, and it was obvious to him that this woman's marriage could not be repaired. Drawing out the relationship would only lengthen the discomfort for both partners and would continue to pose a threat to the emotional stability of the children.

The woman was still young and attractive. "She will marry again," Dr. Montgomery advised, "once she gets her nerves under control and accepts the failure of her marriage. She is dwelling on her troubles too much now, and it is affecting her personality."

Dr. Montgomery said he would keep in touch with the woman and continue to offer help. But if she didn't follow his advice this time, he would tell her not to come back.

"I'm busy, I have so much to do that if people don't listen, then I can't afford to waste my time."

He got up from his desk and went to the doorway, asking the other woman to come in. She hadn't been there before, and she entered hesitantly. She sat down in the chair offered to her by Dr. Montgomery and in broken English explained that she was there for a healing. She pointed to her legs.

Huge discolored veins protruded from her legs in ugly purple masses. They were so painful, she said, she could hardly walk or do her housework. A doctor had told her they should be operated on.

There was no question that she needed help. But Dr. Montgomery could not do the healing. Not in his office. He explained to the woman as gently as he could that he no longer did individual healings.

Individual healing is seen by most medical and legal authorities as bordering on the practice of medicine without a license. To illustrate his point, Dr. Montgomery told the woman about psychic surgeon Antonio C. Agpaoa of the Philippines.

Agpaoa has been credited with hundreds of healings of terminally ill patients. Agpaoa, who has no medical training, effects his cures by the incredible process of pushing his hand into the body of his patient, and removing diseased tissue. The operation is accomplished painlessly, with no anesthesia and no surgical incisions. He merely pushes his hand through the flesh and pokes around until he finds the offending tissue. The psychic incisions heal by themselves.

It is hard to believe, even for the most credible, until one has the opportunity personally to watch an operation or to talk with someone who has been healed. Yet "Tony" and other Philippine psychic surgeons less well known to Americans perform hundreds of successful psychic surgery operations every year.

Plane loads of North Americans have flown to the Philippines for psychic surgery. Yet, when Agpaoa came to the United States in 1968, he was arrested on a federal grand jury indictment from Detroit charging fraud in foreign commerce. The indictment was based on transfer of funds from a bank in Warren, Michigan, to a Canadian bank for a charter flight to the Philippines by psychic surgery patients. Legal minds determined that what Agpaoa claimed was impossible, thus fraud in foreign commerce occurred with the transfer of the $70,000.

Agpaoa jumped bail and returned to the Philippines before his case came up for a scheduled hearing on January 23, 1969.

In 1967, the psychic surgeon had run into trouble with Patrick Ruddy, of the staff of the Illinois Attorney General's Office and with U.S. postal agents. He was forced to leave Chicago.

The woman listened attentively as Dr. Montgomery told her about Agpaoa's difficulties in this country. When he was through talking, she timidly suggested that if Dr. Montgomery would heal her she would keep it quiet, just between the two of them. No one else, she promised, would ever know.

The clergyman-psychic, of course, could not consent to the proposal. Instead, he told her, she should come to the Los Angeles Convention Center in a few days, when he would be presiding at a blessing, healing and deliverance service. If it was in

God's plan, he said, she would be healed at that time. The woman left, disappointed but promising to attend the service.

Four more people had entered the office while he was conferring with the two women. They too were given counseling.

The outer office was finally empty, and Dr. Montgomery had an opportunity to look at his mail. It was more heartening than his first two encounters of the day.

Dr. Montgomery's mail comes from throughout the country, and the problems are as varied as the geographical locations. He is truly a poor man's psychiatrist, who responds to the poignant pleas of his flock with a combination of commonsense counseling, spiritual comfort and psychic insight. Some typical letters, which are on file with this author, follow in the spelling and punctuation of the writers:

Dear Rev. Montgomery.
    I recive your sweet letter. Yes I am so happy to see this new year come in I was so happy to be able to fall on my knee and think the Lord for the many good blessing that he sent upon me. I think God for riseing me new year day giving me my right mine. My grandauther come home to me doing xmas. I had that child every sent she was born and soon as she got big enough to help me my dauther got married. This man want my grandauther from me. He war'nt her father. My family and friends told her it was right for her to take the child from me. So I start writing you. So the child come home to me say she will never leave me anymore. I didn't know what to think but I think you and all who prayed for me and my mother. I so happy to have her here with me. I sure do wish you would visit me in this city.

                                        Mrs. J. G.
                                        Augusta, Georgia

Dear Dr. Montgomery:
    Since I asked you to pray for me my life has taken an upturn. I found a job working in a religious bookstore, and plan to get my own apartment soon to live by myself.
    I am socializing more, and recently met an attractive young lady who seems to be interested in me. She is a Chris-

tian, and moved to this area from the East AFTER you began INCLUDING ME IN YOUR PRAYERS. From one who appreciates your work and spiritual guidance.

M. S.
Evanston, Illinois

Dear Dr. Rev. Montgomery:

Sir, I wrote you about my new apatmunt I am so happy to have it. But now I need money to pay four it, or the landlord say he will thrown me and my family out. I am so happy with Blessing of apatmunt. But I rely need helps now with money to pay. Please pray four me and send me new Blessing. Hurry, I hardly know what to do. Also my husband is laying around with other womens who are bad. The devil is busy in my life and I need your help for my life.

Mrs. D. C. S.
Chicago

Dear Montgomery,

I was so very glad to hear from you . . .

In order to feed my family and pay my bills, I need another part time job, to go along with this full time one, or my career really needs to start moving in the right direction. I've been making tapes and contacting recording co., just trying real hard to help myself. Please increase prayer for me.

Love & peace,

J. W.
Toledo, Ohio

Dr. Montgomery writes personal replies to his correspondents. Some, of course, require no answer. And sometimes he telephones, when an emergency situation exists. Almost none of his correspondents include return postage with their letters. Thus the cost of stamps and telephone is an expensive burden, yet a burden that he accepts as a necessary part of his long-distance ministry.

He jotted notes on a pad as he read the letters. He would refer to them later when typing his replies, after suitable meditation for those correspondents with problems and prayers for all of his church members.

Most of the letters were set aside unopened when he discontinued reading to check with his answering service. There were a half-dozen messages, four from men and women he was counseling.

Another was from Wickliffe and the last was from Phil Barton, a former announcer and reporter with a Los Angeles radio station, who later moved to a job with the Model Cities Agency. Barton had met Dr. Montgomery when he was assigned by his station to interview him. The meeting led to a friendship. Barton eventually became an unofficial, unpaid adviser in public relations to Dr. Montgomery and the church.

Wickliffe had called to confirm a luncheon meeting. Barton left a message to telephone him to iron out a problem concerning the latest issue of *The Guiding Star,* a magazine distributed to members of the church.

Dr. Montgomery telephoned Barton's office and left a message. Barton was out. Meanwhile two more women and a man had entered Montgomery's office and were awaiting counseling, so he telephoned Wickliffe and postponed the luncheon meeting until later in the week. This would be another day when the psychic clergyman skipped lunch.

He was hardly aware of it. The missed meals keep his frame spare, and by keeping his system unclogged with unnecessary food, he is strengthened spiritually for his work. When he is planning absent healing of someone who is critically ill, he fasts for twenty-four hours, taking only a small amount of water or pure fruit or vegetable juice.

Dr. Montgomery motioned the first woman into his office. She was having trouble with her husband. He wasn't giving her household money, because he was losing most of his paycheck gambling. Although they were already deeply in debt, he had bought an expensive new Buick to impress his friends. She told the clergyman that when she complained, her husband beat her. She pushed up the short sleeve of her dress to show her bruised and swollen shoulder, injured when her husband brutally twisted her arm.

The minister told the woman to stop quarreling with her husband, and to get a job. He said to try to keep up the payments on the house, but to let the finance company have the car if her husband was unable to meet the monthly bills. And pray.

Be patient, Montgomery told her, and in time her husband would see the error of his ways and show more responsibility.

Dr. Montgomery said good-by to the woman and called the man in. He was short and balding and talked hesitantly, with a slight lisp. The man was not a member of the Metaphysical Church but came to Dr. Montgomery on the advice of a friend. He was having trouble with his wife.

She wasn't a bad woman, he said, but she was running around with other men, wasn't properly caring for their small son and was letting the house go uncleaned for days at a time. His mother had advised him to throw his wife out.

Would the wife come with him for a joint counseling session, Dr. Montgomery asked? The man didn't know but said he would try to bring her. He left, promising to be in touch by telephone to set up another meeting with or without his wife.

Dr. Montgomery later explained that judging from the man's story there appeared to be little hope for the marriage. But he would not counsel the man either way until he had heard the other side of the story, if possible. A husband and wife rarely give the same account when they are discussing marital difficulties.

It was after 1 P.M. when he ushered the last woman into his office. She was carefully dressed in a becoming beige suit and appeared to be in her early thirties. There were deep frown lines at the edges of her eyes and mouth. Dr. Montgomery had counseled her before.

She was an executive secretary and was having trouble with her job. To be more specific, she was having trouble with another woman who had recently been hired. She told Dr. Montgomery that she believed the newcomer was the boss's mistress and was deliberately harassing her.

The psychic quietly listened until the woman was through talking. Then he leaned back in his chair, closed his eyes and rubbed at his temples. He sat with his eyes closed for a few minutes. The woman patiently waited.

Dr. Montgomery leaned forward, nodding his head. "You would make a good psychic," he said. "This woman you are having trouble with has a romantic relationship with your boss, and they want you to quit so that she can have your job. I would advise you to do so. Quit or seek a transfer."

He explained that even though she could complain to her boss's superior, that it would be her word against his. It would be easy for her boss to argue that she was merely jealous of the other woman, who was younger and very pretty. Even if the younger woman were somehow eliminated from the picture, the boss would be certain to hold a grudge. Working for him would not be pleasant.

It would be far better, Montgomery urged, to look for a job in a different department. Her boss would probably help her and she could leave as a friend instead of as an enemy. The psychic added that he sensed trouble ahead for the couple, and she might even return to her old job in the near future.

The woman wasn't sure she wanted to take the advice. She grumbled that she didn't like being chased out of a job by the boss and his girl friend. But Dr. Montgomery persisted in his decision, and she left, still frowning and upset.

"She will probably go back and pick a fight with the other girl," Dr. Montgomery observed. "Then she will quit or get herself fired. People ask for advice and then they go and do what they want to, anyway."

No one was in the outer office, so he turned again to the stack of letters, shuffling through them until he pulled one from the pile that carried a Michigan postmark. Inside there was a photograph of a woman. She appeared to be in her late forties or early fifties and was grossly overweight.

Dr. Montgomery had heard from the woman before, when she wrote and asked him to help her curb her appetite. Doctors had told her that there was nothing medically wrong with her except her weight. There were no hormonal imbalances. She simply overate. She had put on weight until it became crippling, and she could no longer move around to do her housework. Dr. Montgomery had asked her to mail the photograph.

He removed it from the envelope and placed it on the desk in front of him. He turned the bell on the telephone down and leaned back, tipping his head toward the photograph, and concentrated. As he stared at the picture, he visualized the pounds being stripped away. He formed a mental image of her growing slimmer.

He pictured the woman in his mind, slender and healthy, walking along the street, dancing with her husband and walking through a woods on a spring day. He projected those thoughts to her in Michigan to give her a new image of herself. To be slim and healthy, one must be able to visualize oneself as slim and healthy.

After three or four minutes Dr. Montgomery lifted his head, picked up the picture and replaced it in the envelope, setting it aside. Later, he would write to the woman, remind her to keep visualizing herself as slim and to continue to cut down on her food intake.

Dr. Montgomery looked at his wristwatch. It was ten minutes after three. A client was due at three-fifteen for counseling. He reached for his telephone and dialed long distance to a man in East St. Louis who had been crippled in a construction accident. Dr. Montgomery had been praying for him and sending absent healings.

As he talked with the man, his client came in for the three-fifteen appointment, accompanied by a woman. The man in East St. Louis was feeling better. His pain had subsided, and he was in better spirits than he had been for weeks. Yes, he said, he had felt the healing power of the Holy Spirit. Dr. Montgomery promised to continue working for him, hung up the telephone and walked to the door to greet the man waiting outside.

Before Dr. Montgomery completed his counseling session with the man, the woman friend he brought with him and two other clients scheduled later in the afternoon, it was after 5 P.M. and time to leave the office. He was tired and hungry. He hadn't eaten since early morning, when he boiled two green bananas and a cup of herbal tea. He called his answering service to tell them he was leaving the office, scooped up the unopened letters, his notes and walked out.

Despite his fatigue, he was softly whistling a few minutes later as he turned the wheels of his Cadillac into the curb in front of the ochre-hued adobe apartment complex in Hollywood and parked.

There is a courtyard with a fountain at the entrance to the complex. Inside, his apartment is awash in a happy clutter of magazines, tape cassettes, letters, writing material, shoes and socks. A couple of dozen magazines and newspapers are laid out on the floor in one corner of the room, carefully stacked in rows. Each one has a story, a picture or a mention of Dr. Montgomery, his church or his work.

The apartment is simply furnished, and despite the organized clutter, it is clean. There is a small beige sofa at one end of the front room, a matching easy chair, stereo, a pair of lamps and three small tables. A picture of Christ is on the wall.

There is no liquor cabinet, and there are no ashtrays. "No one will go to hell for sipping a little wine or smoking some cigarettes," Dr. Montgomery concedes. "But drugs inhibit one's psychic ability, so I very seldom indulge. It must be a very special occasion before I will drink a glass of wine."

The kitchen of the apartment is built for efficiency. A stove and small icebox flank a floor cabinet on one side. There is a small breakfast nook. The dishes are washed and neatly stacked.

The apartment has the unmistakable look of a bachelor. The bedroom is neat and the bed carefully made, but the whole atmosphere is strictly masculine. There are no frilly spreads, no cosmetics, no doilies or feminine touches in any of the rooms.

Dr. Montgomery enjoys feminine companionship and dates various women. But his devotion to his work and curious personal habits make it difficult to form lasting relationships. He sometimes has to interrupt dinner dates to make long telephone calls to the sick or other people he has been praying for. At other times when his date has dancing on her mind, or a show or other activities, he has to excuse himself to meditate.

The few hours that he saves for recreation are more likely to be spent showing friends through nearby Disneyland, at a dinner party or at one of Wickliffe's backyard barbecues than in a dance hall.

Dr. Montgomery set his brief case on the floor next to an end table, slid off his shoes, and stretched out on the sofa for a catnap. In fifteen minutes, he was up and in the kitchen, turning on the tap and leaning over to splash cool water on his face. He blotted up the moisture with a towel and was ready to prepare supper. The food that night would be Jamaican. It usually is.

Whistling a calypso tune, he rolled up his sleeves and took about a dozen small silver fish from the refrigerator and placed them into a lightly greased skillet. Turning the heat on low, he allowed the fish to brown slightly before flipping them out and dropping them into a pot to steam.

The fish remained in the pot until they had nearly disintegrated, being reduced to a few small bones. The cook strained the bones from the pot and replaced them with sliced scallions, tomatoes and onions. The concoction was sprinkled with black pepper, and more water was added with butter.

Dr. Montgomery's Jamaican fish tea was ready to eat. A tin of "ackee," an imported West Indian vegetable, was added to complete the meal.

After the meal was eaten and the dishes washed, another two hours were spent answering mail. Then thirty minutes were devoted to reading the Bible. Reading of the Bible, written in parables as it is and requiring interpretation, stimulates the mind. Dr. Montgomery reads it every day.

He was finally ready to lead his flock into the Golden Room. He meditates each evening and each morning, projecting thoughts of a huge Golden Room, radiating with healing comforting light.

Dr. Montgomery began his Golden Room meditations after he was told clairaudiently to: "Go ye and prepare a method for going into the silence."

The silence, of course, means meditation. The Golden Room was selected after he was reminded, during meditation, of King Solomon's Golden Temple.

Dr. Montgomery carries thoughts with him into his Golden Room of all those from whom he has received correspondence and for whom he is working. There is general meditation on good things for them.

Messages sometimes come to him in the Golden Room. A picture may flash briefly into his consciousness of a train wreck, of an assassination or of a government being toppled. When this happens he will later go into trance or occasionally into soul travel to seek more information.

It was 11 P.M. when the psychic left his Golden Room, and time for bed. He slept for three hours before getting up again and working until 4 A.M. He slept another two hours.

The new day was begun at 6 A.M. with prayers and a cold bath. As a boy in Jamaica he developed the habit of bathing each day in cool invigorating water. And he developed the habit of prayer.

8

Do It Yourself

MEDITATION IN THE MORNING AND AT NIGHT REFRESHES
Dr. Montgomery in mind and spirit.

Despite his long hours and the pressure of carrying on his
ministry-by-mail, lectures, healing seminars and work with the
needy, Dr. Montgomery seldom is sick.

When others are sick and come to him for help, he heals
with prayer and healing energy. When he is threatened by illness himself, he heals through prayer, meditation and the power
of the mind.

Mind control, autosuggestion, self-hypnosis, mental imagery,
creative visualization—whatever it is called is not important.
What IS Important is the result. Self-healing through control of
his own mind and body.

Dr. Montgomery heals himself with mind control, and so
can you. Using only the power of your own mind, reinforced by
prayer if you wish, you can visualize a healthy body and prevent
disease or heal yourself if illness already is present.

One of the most dramatic and scientifically documented examples of mind-over-matter healing was recounted at the Acad-

emy of Parapsychology and Medicine's 1975 conference in Tucson.

There, Dr. Carl Simonton and his wife, Stephanie, told of the work at their cancer control clinic in Fort Worth, Texas, where terminally ill patients are taught to treat themselves with mental imagery while they are undergoing conventional healing with radiation, medication or surgery.

Their success rate with patients virtually written off as hopeless by the medical community if treated with only the traditional modalities appears miraculous. It is more than two and a half times the national average for terminal patients.

During a two-year study of 152 patients treated by Dr. Simonton while he was chief of radiation therapy at Travis Air Force Base in California, marked relief of symptoms and dramatic improvement was shown by twenty patients whose attitudes were positive and co-operative. Some had eliminated all signs of cancer. There was no improvement shown in sixty-five patients who were negative and non-co-operative. The other sixty-seven patients showed general improvement and relief and included sixty-five who almost always followed instructions and two who did not.

Dr. Simonton provides the conventional medical treatment and is assisted by his wife, a lay therapist, in adminstering the supportive therapy. She usually leads the patients in group therapy, often including family members and close friends. The Simontons teach their patients to activate the natural immunological processes within their own bodies to help in the healing. They teach the patients to meditate and visualize the cancer cells being destroyed.

Mrs. Simonton explained that patients are instructed to meditate daily for fifteen minutes in the morning, at noon and before going to bed. The first few minutes are devoted to relaxation, followed by a minute's visualization of a pleasing outdoors scene.

Then it is time for the key to the exercise, visualizing the tumor itself. As the patient watches the tumor with his mind's eye, he imagines an army of white blood cells arriving and swarming over the cancer. In his imagery, he sees malignant cells, already weakened or killed by radiation from the cobalt machine, or by other conventional treatment, being carried away.

Attitudes and personal character traits of patients, as well as the support of family and close friends, appear to be vital factors in their ability to defeat the malignancies.

Stephanie Simonton told of a sixty-one-year-old patient with advanced throat cancer who was given only a 5 per cent chance of survival when he came to them. During his illness he had dropped from 135 to ninety-five pounds and could barely swallow his own saliva.

A strong-willed man, he accepted explanations of the body's cancer-immune mechanisms and ability to heal itself as sensible. He undertook the unconventional treatment program eagerly and with a positive attitude, missing only one meditative session in the seven weeks of treatment.

He recovered, and more than five years later, Mrs. Simonton reported, he was still doing well. Moreover, using the same relaxation-visualization techniques, he relieved an arthritic condition that had preceded the cancer and had overcome sexual impotence that had plagued him for more than twenty years.

The Simontons have observed a strong link between stress situations, such as loss of a loved one through death, loss of a job and forced retirement, with development of cancer. Housewives in their forties who suddenly find themselves with their children grown up and away from home experience a similar shock or stress situation and can be another example of the cancer-prone, Mrs. Simonton said.

The origins of more than 80 per cent of illness have psychosomatic roots, so if the mind can help cause cancer, why can it not also be used to help cure cancer? the Simontons reasoned.

Dr. Montgomery advises those who are ill to use a combination of approaches similar to those utilized by the Simontons before approaching psychic or faith healers: conventional medicine reinforced by self-healing through creative visualization. As a clergyman, of course, he recommends adding the power of prayer.

"There is a healing force. Describe it as an electromagnetic field or whatever you like, but it comes directly from God," he said. So God should not be left out.

"It is God's plan that his children be healthy. Illness occurs when something goes wrong with the plan, and when that happens, it is time to use your mind, meditation and prayer to do God's own healing."

When Dr. Montgomery was being interviewed for this book, he spent several hours one day in July seated next to the blowing fan of an air conditioner in the Hollywood Holiday Inn. When he left that evening for his apartment, his eyes were red and watering and he was sniffling and rubbing at his nose with a handkerchief.

The next morning he showed up, looking as fresh as the white carnation in his lapel. His eyes were clear, there were no sniffles, and as he talked in his deep, resonant Jamaican dialect there was no sign of hoarseness or of a cold. But my eyes were moist with tears, my nose was running and my throat was raw.

Dr. Montgomery had done a self-healing. I had not.

The self-healing was simple. "All I did," he told me, "was to meditate strongly when I realized that a cold was beginning to manifest itself. I meditated and told myself that no cold would prevent me from meeting you today to continue with our work. In other words, I shut the question of illness or of a cold out of my mind completely. I wouldn't have it."

When he awakened the morning after his long exposure to the air conditioner, he sneezed three or four times during the first couple of hours. That was the end of the sneezing and the end of the fledgling cold. He had taken no aspirin, no vitamin C, no hot whiskey toddies or drugstore remedies. He defeated the cold with the power of his mind.

Compared to cancer, a cold may appear insignificant. But while medical science has developed methods of successfully treating some cancer, it has not yet come up with a cure for the common cold. And it never will, as Dr. Montgomery explains in a later chapter.

"Your mind can make you sick, and your mind can make you well," he says, encapsulating what was to be an underlying theme of the Tucson conference a few months later.

Dr. Montgomery has increasingly passed on his self-healing techniques to others as his far-flung congregation and his responsibilities have grown. Psychic healers and others touched by God have healing missions to carry out, he believes, but they also have a responsibility to teach others to heal themselves. Other healers have come to the same conclusion.

Rosita Rodriguez, of Oak Park, Illinois, a suburb of Chicago, is one of those. She and her associate, Tom Hanauer, are students of Tony Agpaoa, and although they can perform psychic surgery, insist that they do not do so in this country because of laws against the practice.

Instead, they cure with laying on of hands and magnetism. (Hanauer, in the summer of 1975, vividly demonstrated the efficacy of his skill by healing a recurring back injury of mine with a soothing massage and laying on of hands.)

But both Mrs. Rodriguez and Hanauer appear to be as enthusiastic about the potential of their classes in philosophy and seminars in self-healing as in the individual healings they now perform.

"Healing has limits," Mrs. Rodriguez explained. "If you don't get at the source of what is causing the trouble, your patients will just come back in a short time with something else wrong with them. We believe that almost all illness is caused at the emotional level, so patients must be taught to heal their emotional and spiritual environment while healing their bodies.

"I have thought for a long time that when we totally depend on someone else to heal us, we are leaving out the intellect and our own will. And that is what total health depends on, exercising intellect and our own free will. We've found that out in our own family. No one here ever gets sick anymore."

The Oak Park healers teach their system of environmental control for health and happiness at forty-five-hour seminars scheduled on consecutive weekends during months when they are not traveling or occupied with other responsibilities.

"People do heal themselves in the seminar," Mrs. Rodriguez said. "But many other things also happen to them. They become more assertive, they earn more money, their human relations improve. The whole entity is touched, not just the physical body."

Dr. Montgomery agrees with the idea of creating a healthy mental and spiritual environment for one's self to prevent disease and to remain healthy. And he concurs that once this environment is created, it is beneficial in all areas of one's life.

Once while working at his office, he answered his telephone, and it was a woman in Fort Worth, Texas. She obviously was distraught. Her voice was shrill and frightened. Physicians had given up on her, and she was in so much pain she didn't know what to do, she said. She had written to Dr. Montgomery, asking for help, but hadn't received a reply.

He didn't remember receiving her letter, and her name and address were not familiar. "When was the letter mailed?" he asked.

"Four days ago."

The psychic healer spread the pile of mail on his desk and shuffled through the letters. In a few moments he found a letter with a Fort Worth postmark. It was from the woman.

In the letter she complained that she was suffering from emphysema, congestion, bursitis in the left shoulder and arthritis in one knee. She could hardly breathe and couldn't work at her job on the production line of a local factory. She said she was afraid of doctors and medication.

Dr. Montgomery picked the phone up and told the woman that he had found her letter and read it. He was interrupted before he could continue.

Breathing with difficulty as she became more agitated, the woman gasped that she was in her late thirties, single and had no close relatives or friends. Although she believed strongly in religion and the Holy Spirit, she did not belong to a church and had no one now to depend on but Dr. Montgomery. She started to cry.

Dr. Montgomery talked to her, soothing her, and when she stopped crying, he explained that he would send her a healing. But she must also help herself.

They would work the healing together, he explained. To begin with, she should lock her door, then turn the lights down and sit up in her bed or in a chair and meditate on her medical problems clearing up. She had never heard the word "meditate" before.

"Just concentrate on being immediately relieved of your problem. Close your eyes and think hard about all the illness, all the pain, leaving your body. See yourself as healthy, smiling and feeling good," he said.

As she meditated, he said, he would project a visual image of good health for her so that their combined minds and thoughts would create a strong healing vibration. "Begin meditating in five minutes," he said, and hung the telephone up.

He waited five minutes and began his projection of good health for the woman, visualizing the pain and illness draining from her body and the fear leaving her mind. After fifteen minutes he reached for the telephone and dialed her number.

"How do you feel?" he asked.

"Fine, just fine," she chirped. "I'm going to get dressed and go to work."

Dr. Montgomery was startled by the rapid healing, but he didn't lose his composure. He told the woman that he was delighted that the healing had worked so completely and quickly but cautioned her that healings sometimes require a little backup work. He advised her not to return to her job immediately, at least not that day.

He suggested instead that she go to a store and buy three white candles. He instructed her to put the candles on a dresser in her bedroom and to light them at the same time each morning for one week, letting them burn for fifteen minutes at a time.

Dr. Montgomery explained that the candles symbolized:

—Faith in herself, and faith that she could be healed through God's power.

—Hope, that she may be healed of all her ailments, physical, mental and emotional, so that her life might take on new meaning.

—Charity, so that she did not forget to send at least three dollars per month to the church to help maintain the ministry.

The woman must have burned only the first two candles, because Dr. Montgomery never heard from her again.

"That's typical," he mused. "When they call back or write, they're usually still having problems. When everything is going good, I never hear from them."

Even though she overlooked charity in complying with his advice, Dr. Montgomery mailed more detailed instructions to her explaining how to visualize her ailments away and to project a self-image of good health.

Instructions explaining how to improve her spiritual and physical life through daily periods of general meditation were also included.

General meditation is different than the combined meditative-visualization process recommended to the woman to alleviate her illness and distress. In general meditation, which shall be referred to simply as meditation from this point on, the goal is to become aware of the union between the meditator and all things. For the Christian, Dr. Montgomery says, the goal should be one of unifying with the Holy Spirit of Christ.

Different psychics use different meditation techniques, and most jealously guard their own particular method from others. But because Dr. Montgomery sees all meditation properly carried out as leading to greater awareness and a closer tie with the Holy Spirit, he believes his technique should be shared.

Because of his heightened psychic awareness, the techniques he uses for himself differ slightly from those he prescribes for others. Almost none of his congregation have been trained or are experienced in meditation, so he tailors the instruction for the individual. Yet the basics remain the same.

He recommends at least two meditation sessions of about fifteen minutes each day, preferably early morning and in the evening. Before beginning, he says, one should spend a few minutes reading the Bible. (If an individual is not Christian, other religious writings, poetry, philosophy or listening to inspirational music will do.)

Some people find that a lighted candle is a helpful prop for meditating, but Dr. Montgomery says that it is not necessary. One can slip into the meditative state quite easily without props merely by following his simple instructions. Nor does he use a "mantra," a word constantly repeated either aloud or mentally until it drives all other thoughts from the mind. The mantra is popularly used in Eastern religions and meditative systems.

Dr. Montgomery usually does his evening meditation in bed, but not everyone can stay awake after assuming a horizontal position. So he recommends instead that the meditator use any sitting position that is comfortable, so long as the spine is kept straight.

(Some meditation systems are very specific about posture and may require that the meditator assume the lotus position. This means the right foot should be pressed against the left thigh, the left foot pressed against the right thigh and the hands folded in the lap with thumbs touching. Of course, the back must be straight.)

Once seated comfortably, Dr. Montgomery says, the meditator should either fold the hands in the lap with the thumbs lightly touching or let them lie gently in the lap, palms up. A little experimentation will soon reveal which is the most effective position for the individual.

Before beginning meditation, one should first create a seal of protection. "Do this before you enter any phase of meditation, because when you meditate you enter a completely new dimension, where the physical is no longer attuned to the safety of the individual," Dr. Montgomery explains. "And for the smooth aligning of the person's thought, sealing is very important.

"Meditating is like going into a cave. Before going in there, you should be sure that you can find your way out again. You prepare yourself before venturing inside a cave. It is the same way with meditation.

"The sealing process is simple. Visualize in the invisible psychic eye that is in the center of your forehead just above the bridge of the nose divine protection enveloping you like a blanket. See a divine protective mantle surrounding you like: 'On my journey, I will be protected. No harm will come to me, because I am being protected by God.'"

When you feel the protection around you, it is time to begin meditation itself. Begin by visualizing a single thought, word or form. Preferably the image or thought should be of the Bible, Christ, the Cross or some other spiritual symbol that has importance to you. The eyes can be open or closed, but for the beginner—unless a candle or physical prop is used—it is usually easier to work with eyes closed.

Fix the image in your mind. If your thoughts begin to wander off, and they will if you are inexperienced, gently draw them back. You will be amazed at how difficult it is at first to keep your mind from roaming about on its own, intruding with thoughts of your job, that picnic you've been planning, the strange ping that has just developed in your car engine or the faint lyrics of a song being played on a radio next door.

But stick with it. The longer you meditate, the more disciplined your mind will become and the easier it will be to shut out distracting thoughts and sounds.

After about eight or ten minutes of focusing on the image you have chosen and anchoring it in your mind to the best of your ability, you will have begun to build up energy that you can utilize in the next step.

It will be time then to release your mind and let the thoughts flow freely. This will be the period of your meditation when you receive messages. You will be tapping the power of your subconscious, and pictures or symbols may come into your mind. Or a thought may just suddenly appear there. You may hear voices. The solution to problems that you thought were unsolvable may occur to you all at once.

Finally, it will be time to end the meditative session and close off your altered state of receptiveness to retain that which you have already received and to lock out disturbing influences from others.

Simply concentrate on a protective shield closing around you and feel the security that comes with knowing that you will not be bothered by someone else's bad vibes.

Don't be disappointed if it takes a while before you begin getting results from your meditation. A feeling of well-being should be noticeable first. It will take a while longer for other benefits of your new consciousness expanding to begin to show up.

Probably, you will begin to notice higher developed psychic powers. You will have more and stronger hunches. You will have premonitions of coming events. Other people's vibrations will come through to you more strongly. Pay attention. It is your new awareness. Your subconsciousness is breaking through.

Do not be afraid of meditation or the expanded consciousness it leads to. The level of meditation outlined by Dr. Montgomery here for others is not trance and there is no danger of accidentally slipping into trance while meditating. You will not lose consciousness, only expand it.

Dr. Montgomery says meditation can be effectively used in conjunction with prayer, but should not be used instead of or confused with prayer. General meditation does not involve petitioning or offering thanksgiving to divine powers, and thus is not like most kinds of prayer.

"Prayer is just a communication with the Divinity," Dr. Montgomery says. "And as Christians we are able to contact the Holy Spirit or invoke the guidance of God or Christ with prayer. You lift your thoughts and ask the Lord to be with you and to administer to your physical and spiritual needs.

"You do not need a building to pray in, no church, synagogue, shrine or temple. You can pray anywhere: walking down a street, driving along a freeway, aboard an airplane, and anything that you ask for can be realized, anything at all."

Prayer need not be long, elaborate or loud, he says. A few seconds of silent petitioning or thanksgiving is all that is needed, but it must come from the heart and be offered with faith. "The Bible says not to pray like the publicans do, but to pray silently. Just be resolute, and petition God directly.

"Christ, Who was resurrected, said: 'Ask, and it shall be given you. Seek, and you shall find.' "

Christ's resurrection is proof of the validity of reincarnation, Dr. Montgomery says. "Christ's resurrection is the most dramatic reincarnation in the Bible. He died on the Cross, and three days later He walked again. Christ said that when He died, He would come back. And that is exactly what He meant. He was there in the image and form that had previously been His.

"Did Christ die? Yes! Did He return? Yes! So I'm saying that after you die, you return. Where then is the conflict between what I am saying and Christianity?" he asks.

Christ, of course, returned in the same form He had before the crucifixion, and the Eastern religions teach, as well, that one does not come back in the same body or with the same exact physical appearance. Christ's more dramatic return was accomplished to show an example to all mankind, says Dr. Montgomery.

"Any of the rest of us may return as male or female, as another human being," he says. "But Christ's resurrection was the classic example. He was opening the eyes of everyone, telling them that when you die, that you do return."

Dr. Montgomery has seen personal proof of reincarnation, traveling the soul planes, and differs with other Christian theologians who take a more fundamentalist view of the soul. Orthodox Christianity teaches that after physical death the soul lives only one lifetime on this plane before passing into purgatory, heaven or hell.

Most Eastern religions, as well as many other faiths around the world, teach instead the idea of a progression of lives, based on the premise that more than one life is needed to achieve a sufficient state of perfection to move permanently to a higher level of existence.

As previously mentioned, Dr. Montgomery traces his spiritual genealogy to King Solomon and the Queen of Sheba. He is certain that his love of uniforms and pomp, evidenced by his experience with marching bands, the Jamaican Home Guard and the national police force are holdovers from that previous existence.

As a bastard son of King Solomon and the Queen of Sheba, he fell in love with the brilliance of the royal court. His soul retained that love of ostentation, flourish and glitter. It also retained qualities passed on to him by his earthly parents in that lifetime, forging a direct physical link to the ancient potentates.

Dr. Montgomery credits much of his ability as a child to advise adults on matters that were far too complex for his juvenile understanding to his former physical relationship with King Solomon. Although it changes bodies the human soul retains qualities from previous lifetimes that show up in many ways and affect the new individual that the old soul and new physical body have become.

The human soul must continue the process of reincarnation through what Dr. Montgomery refers to as "six innings." An inning, he explains, lasts from 100 years to a millennium.

Most religious writings refer many times to reincarnation. The Bhagavad-Gita, the most widely known of Hindu religious writings, talks of the body as a garment. It is shed when it is worn out, and the soul then dons a new garment.

The Bible, too, has its references to the progression of lives that is reincarnation. One, which Dr. Montgomery quotes from St. Matthew 9:17 says:

> Neither do men put new wine into old bottles:
> Else the bottles break,
> And the wine runneth out,
> And the bottles perish:
> But they put new wine into new bottles,
> And both are preserved.

PART 3

Tomorrow

1

The Years Ahead

THE MOST DRAMATIC DEVELOPMENT IN THE HISTORY OF mankind before the year 2000 will be contact and war with creatures from other worlds.

Changes in family life, business, medicine and other areas of interest to man in the next quarter of a century, revolutionary though they will be, will pale when compared to man's violent meeting with more highly evolved and technologically advanced beings.

Calling on his powers of trance-induced vision and soul travel, Dr. Montgomery learned that the mystery of the UFO phenomena will be solved with disclosure that they are craft piloted by creatures from outer space and from beneath the Atlantic Ocean.

"It should not be surprising that there are other intelligent life forms besides those of us who inhabit the surface of the earth," Dr. Montgomery said. "God is mighty and powerful, so what would make it so impossible for Him to perform His feat of creation somewhere else?"

Most Americans do not now believe that it is impossible that life exists in other worlds. As early as 1973, a Gallup Poll disclosed that 15 million Americans, 11 per cent of the adult population, claimed to have seen a UFO. And 51 per cent of the population believed that UFOs are real, that they are not swamp gas or the product of someone's imagination.

Astronaut John W. Young, an *Apollo XVI* crew member and the ninth man to walk on the moon, was quoted by the Associated Press on November 27, 1973, as saying that there is practically no chance that extraterrestrial life does not exist.

"If you bet against it, you'd be betting against an almost sure thing," he was quoted. "There are so many stars that it's mathematically improbable that there aren't other life sources in the universe."

Major world governments are aware of the origin of UFOs, said Dr. Montgomery, but are covering up information to prevent panic. "People are afraid of what they do not understand, and an announcement that flying saucers are indeed piloted by creatures from outer space or from below the surface of the earth would create terrible alarm, especially when the governments of the world are forced to admit, as they will be, that they do not know how to deal with these other beings."

Unfortunately, Dr. Montgomery said, shortly before the year 2000, extraterrestrial beings will launch an attack on underground nuclear weapon emplacements and stockpile sites. The United States, Russia, China, Israel, India, France, Great Britain and other nations with nuclear weapons will be targets.

An attack could also come from the civilization below the area of the South Atlantic commonly referred to as the Bermuda Triangle. But Dr. Montgomery saw a good likelihood that man will be able to use free will to prevent a clash with the hairy, bearlike undersea beings after a peaceful contact is made.

"They could offer much to us, but they prefer to live their own lives and let us destroy ourselves so long as we do not bother them," he said. "But as long as man continues to fly airplanes and sail ships through the so-called triangle between Bermuda, Miami and Puerto Rico, the craft will continue to be sucked down by a powerful electromagnetic field."

The extraterrestrials pose a more serious threat. But even though they will war on earth, they will not annihilate mankind.

The outer-space beings from a world many light-years beyond our galaxy are so vastly superior to us in intelligence and technology that their attitudes toward men are completely amoral. They are content, live hundreds of years, have no war, illness or hunger and have no special desire to injure—or serve—humanity.

As we near the capability of intergalactic travel and develop more sophisticated armaments, however, they will be forced to eliminate our weapons, which have both the potential of harming them and of destroying the earth itself. Thus they will bombard the underground armament stockpiles and destroy them with cosmic rockets.

Millions of people will be killed in the assault, not because they are deliberate targets, but merely because they are in the way and because the extraterrestrials see no special reasons to prevent deaths. When the weapon stockpiles have been destroyed, the attacks will cease.

In his book *UFOs: Interplanetary Visitors,* Raymond E. Fowler quotes a statement by General Douglas MacArthur that agrees with Dr. Montgomery's prophecy. The general warned that:

> The nations of the world will have to unite, for the next war will be an interplanetary war. The nations of the earth must someday make a common front against attack by people from other planets.[1]

RELIGION

The knowledge that UFOs are piloted by alien creatures will have an uncontestable impact on religion, shaking the beliefs of millions and strengthening the faith of others. Some will begin to worship the beings from space, much as more primitive civilizations on earth have at times in the past identified more technologically advanced visitors as gods.

Fowler recalled in his book that the Spaniard Cortez was helped to conquer the Aztecs because they mistook him for a god. Once the Indians were conquered, the Spaniards quickly forced them to accept Roman Catholicism.

Dr. Montgomery foresaw no such intergalactic missionary effort on the part of the extraterrestrials. "Does man try to convert cattle, chickens or antelope to his religions?" he asked. "No. There is no way animals with the limitations of their intelligence could grasp such concepts. And the extraterrestrials will look upon us in much the same way."

Religion will be greatly affected by the aliens, but even before that, Dr. Montgomery foresaw significant changes in store.

The large traditional religions such as Christianity, Buddhism and Islam have changed so greatly that they are no longer meaningful to many worshipers. Consequently, Dr. Montgomery learned, smaller sects and cults will continue to proliferate.

"Churches today are too institutionalized. Going to church is like reading a book, and this is no longer acceptable, especially to the younger people," he said. "Hundreds of new religious sects will emerge in this country, and thousands elsewhere in the world, each attracting its own little group of followers. Some, of course, will become quite large, but even those will be constantly changing. They will be in constant flux, with new cults splitting off from the old as each individual searches for the path best suited to himself.

"Organized religion as we know it today in this country will have received its death blow in fifteen years."

Dr. Montgomery did not say man will no longer be religious. The opposite is, in fact, true. But man will look more inside himself for answers, and as he becomes more in touch with the spiritual and psychic world, individual interpretation of developments will lead to a multitude of approaches to the Divinity.

Western man will also throw off much of the guilt fostered by traditional Christianity and will use religion to obtain the best from this life—including material things—as well as to worship the Creator, Dr. Montgomery predicted. "God created the world for every man, woman and child to enjoy. And the church should be the first to teach its followers how to obtain the best that life has to offer. There is no sin attached to being happy."

Dr. Montgomery saw the rift widening between the Pope and the priests of the Roman Catholic Church over the rule of celibacy. Priests will resign from the clergy in large numbers to protest the restriction on marriage.

The issue will finally be resolved by a new pontifical law, permitting marriage three years after ordination into the priesthood.

DISCOVERIES AND INVENTIONS

The remains of Noah's Ark will be found by a combined United States, Canadian and Japanese expedition. The Yeti, or Abominable Snowman, will also be sighted, and photographs will be taken of it. Although the photographs will prove the Yeti's existence, it will again elude capture.

A device will be invented that can locate underwater treasures as small as a pin at a distance of 3,000 feet. The invention will be of vital interest to the United States Navy, which will develop it for use in underwater warfare and to locate and retrieve sunken submarines and surface craft.

FAMILY LIFE

Aggravated by the disturbing influence of television, home life will further disintegrate as communication breaks down almost completely between family members. Older people will live by themselves or in nursing homes provided or supported by the government, as they are shunned by relatives.

Nationwide child care centers and summer camps for children will be established by the government. The facilities will be provided in response to pressure from parents who cannot control their children or who do not wish to take the responsibility for raising them.

POPULATION

Despite efforts of groups alarmed at overpopulation, the birth rate will soar in this country. Relaxation of old moral codes

will permit teen-agers as young as fifteen to live together openly
without the sanction of marriage, and many babies will be born.
"The government will be taking care of the babies, no responsibility will be placed on the teen-age parents, and there will be
no onus attached to unwed parenthood, so contraceptives and
other methods of birth control will be largely ignored," Dr.
Montgomery learned.

MEDICINE

Birth control pills will be banned by the Federal Drug Administration after it is confirmed that continued use contributes
to impaired eyesight in babies and cancer of the uterus in
mothers.

Heart transplant operations will be abolished in the United
States in favor of other methods of treatment. Too many trans-
plants will fail, and there will be a plethora of malpractice suits
against doctors and hospitals by survivors of heart recipients who
have died.

A popular drug now used for treatment of diabetics will be
banned. It will be ascertained that patients using the drug
develop complications leading to an early death.

There will be no medicine developed that will cure the common cold. A cold, said Dr. Montgomery, is an indication that the
body needs rest and that one is not treating the body, mind and
spirit properly. "When one has a cold," he said, "it is time to
meditate and to look into one's inner self—to come back to the
mind." Development of cold is also the body's way of throwing
off impurities, so seeking a cure is a waste of time, he said.

Using the power of the mind is, of course, the best way to
treat a cold. But for those who prefer other approaches, Dr.
Montgomery recommended inhaling cold tap water through the
nostrils to chase a head cold.

"In Jamaica, people who get a cold merely go into the garden or into the bushes and pick three leaves from the Tree of
Life. They wash the leaves, sprinkle them with salt, chew them
and suck the juice. In twenty-four hours," he said, "the cold is
gone."

ECONOMY

High interest rates and rising costs of housing will force the government to subsidize dwellings for families with moderate income. Production of steel, autos and electrical power will drop.

Businesses will become larger in this country, as government controls against monopoly and huge cartels are relaxed. Some small businesses will survive, but their services or products must be outstanding and their management superior to compete with the technological and financial advantages of big business.

Computerization and mechanization will throw millions of workers out of jobs, fostering resentment against government and the wealthy. Only a select few will have jobs, and others will be supported by welfare programs. Unemployed, the great mass of people will become lazy and resentful. Plots and mini-revolutions against the government will be undertaken.

GOVERNMENT

Politicians will continue to wield power but will have little respect from the people they represent. The populace will be apathetic about politics, and officials will be elected on the vote of only a handful of those qualified to cast ballots.

TAXES

Taxes will soar as the government assumes responsibility for more and more services at home and spends billions of dollars propping up weak foreign governments friendly to this country with financial aid and arms.

CRIME

Frustration with idleness and loss of a sense of personal worth, high taxes and disillusionment in our leadership will further spiral the already high crime rate. Bank robberies, homicides, major thefts and shoplifting will rise drastically. But the most dramatic and frightening increase will be in kidnapping.

The death penalty will be reinstated in most areas of the United States for kidnapping, murder and certain types of assault or threat with a deadly weapon in the commission of crime.

RACE RELATIONS

Racial violence will flare and worsen in England, as mobs of young people between the ages of twelve and thirteen band together to attack non-whites. Pakistanis will be especially singled out for beatings. Non-whites will arm themselves with clubs, knives and other weapons and group together to retaliate.

Violence between Catholics and Protestants in Northern Ireland will escalate. Both sides will acquire large amounts of arms and ammunition, and casualties from the ensuing clashes will be high.

2

The Year 2000:
An Astral Visit

WHAT WILL LIFE BE LIKE AT THE BEGINNING OF THE twenty-first century? Will life improve or decline? What will man do and think? How will he survive? To divine answers to these and many other questions about the future, Dr. Montgomery entered into soul travel to visit the twenty-first century. Here are his observations:

WORLD POPULATION

Population will continue to climb in the year 2000, but whites and non-whites will work together for one common purpose—unity among all men. The leading world governments will pool their technological resources in order to find new sources of energy through atomic and solar power. The people of the earth still will be troubled with power shortages.

CLOTHING

We will not be wearing clothes as they appear today. Instead, garments will be designed to be worn for long periods without being changed. For years, scientists have known that too much exposure to the sun causes skin cancer. By the year 2000, they will realize that solar rays debilitate the human body, interfere with general health and shorten our life-span.

Consequently, they will devise garments that cleanse the body when worn. These will be close-fitting suits, much like the space suits pictured in science fiction movies. Air and gases will pass through the fabric and clean the skin.

The uni-sex look will be common, with males and females dressing alike. But at first not everyone will adopt the new clothing styles because there will be no laws requiring them to. These individuals will continue to bathe as they do now, swim and sunbathe. Eventually, however, they will compare the lengths of their lives with the lives of clothing conformists and conclude that the new garments promote longevity.

The fabric will be made in Japan from synthetics and will be good in any weather. The suits will be worn for six months without a change, and the people wearing them can bathe without disrobing, while driving their car or walking along the street.

Men and Women

The relationship between men and women will be wretched and full of discord and jealousy by the year 2000. The government and many private organizations will try to force certain practices and life-styles on women under the direction of women's liberation groups. But millions of men and women will protest. They will continue to insist that a woman's place is in the home as the center of the family, and that her job is to raise the children and to see to their needs and those of her husband.

Many women influenced by the liberationists will refuse to share bedrooms with their husbands. Men, thus cut off from normal relationships with their wives, will react by seeking out more loving women, and the institution of marriage will be temporarily crippled. Family life will be thrown into turmoil.

A re-evaluation of male-female relationships and family will occur as time progresses, however, and radical feminism will eventually lose. The world will return to the family system of the past and women will resume the role of homemaker. They will no longer seek traditionally masculine jobs as construction workers, race car drivers or be destructive to family life. Millions of women will have been diverted from true female pursuits during the period of disruption, but others will have retained their roles of lovers, wives and mothers.

Beyond the year 2000, people will begin to change physically. They will become tall, slender and more symmetrical in shape because of altered diets. People will become so slender that much unnatural strain on their hearts will be alleviated and they will be healthier. Heart attacks will be virtually eliminated.

TRANSPORTATION

A different form of travel craft will be used in the twenty-first century. People will be required to obtain federal drivers' licenses to pilot flying discs, which will travel 500 to 600 miles per hour. They will be called astro-hover-cars.

In their infancy, these craft will seat only three or four passengers. But further development will expand their capacity to eight to ten people. They will emit a slight humming sound and will be able to fly in any direction, much like a helicopter, but with more maneuverability, more grace and ease. When not in use, they will be stored in garages, taking up little more space than bicycles.

The United States and Russia will build them initially, but other technologically advanced countries will also begin their manufacture later. These craft will not be usable for space flights, but they will greatly cut time spent in earth travel. Threatened with loss of their passenger business, airlines will oppose use of the astro-hover-cars, but the opposition will be overcome. Beyond the year 2000, older children will be piloting their own craft, much as they ride bicycles today. The astro-hover-cars will be pollution free.

ECOLOGY

Pollution from automotive exhausts and other sources will become much worse before development of the astro-hover-cars.

The air over cities such as Los Angeles, Dallas, Detroit, and Gary, Indiana, will become so dirty and filled with dangerous chemicals that older people and those suffering from lung disorders will have to wear gas masks.

Ecologists will have failed in their belated efforts to save the environment. Much plant and animal life will have been destroyed. People who continue to eat vegetables and animal products instead of algae and new synthetic foods developed in laboratories will absorb poisonous chemicals directly into their system and their lives will be shortened. Man will develop new diseases related to pollution.

The Atlantic and Pacific oceans are already being choked to death by industrial waste, and the Mediterranean Sea, the Caribbean and the Antarctic and Indian oceans are beginning to be adversely affected by pollution. Valuable marine life is being destroyed and the balance of nature irretrievably altered.

Efforts by the U. S. Department of Agriculture to foster improvements in beef stock, fatten calves more effectively and step up all farm production will be frustrated. The soil will soon become so contaminated from insecticides and other pollutants that animals which subsist on grass will sicken and die.

Unlike man, almost all domestic animals will be adversely affected by the contaminated food and by science's inability to develop adequate substitutes. Racehorses will be debilitated by necessary dietary changes and will no longer have the strength and stamina they are bred for. The population of dogs and cats will dwindle after they are deprived of meat and milk. Most wild animals will have become extinct as a result of pollution and the steady encroachment of man on their habitats.

The world we now live in is doomed unless, using free will, man takes immediate steps to eradicate nuclear testing and weaponry and ends his widespread pollution. The United States and Russia will step up their space programs, seeking new planets suitable for colonization, as the earth gradually dies.

Technology and Space

Space travel by the year 2000 will be accomplished on a wide scale by soul travel as well as with spacecraft. Humans ev-

erywhere will become proficient soul travelers and will undertake expeditions from the privacy of their own bedrooms. This
process of the mind and spirit will be taught in schools and
universities.

3

America and the World of Tomorrow

THE BEGINNING OF THE END

SWEEPING CHANGES WILL OCCUR IN WORLD LEADERSHIP by the year 2000 and beyond. As the twenty-first century opens, it will mark the beginning of the end for the United States as a world power.

Like many other nations before it, the United States will decline in power after 200 years of strength and world dominance. Corruption among politicians and strikes by police, doctors, nurses, airline pilots and teachers will increase. Eventually, the government will disregard completely the desires and needs of its citizens.

Crime will become so common that many families will live in fortresses protected by electronic gates. No one will be able to find safety at home or elsewhere. Extensive unemployment will cause many people to break the law to obtain better food and possessions.

Daylight store robberies will commonly occur, with thieves clearing off shelves and shooting indiscriminately at anyone nearby.

A class of criminals will emerge that will specialize in the robbing of banks, attempting to justify politically its actions by labeling banks as symbols of oppression.

In response, banks will institute a protective system for employees who handle cash, and tellers will be seen only on closed-circuit television. The only employees who will work personally with the public will be secretaries and clerks who take employment applications and open or close accounts and workers in the trust and loan sections. All will be armed or closely guarded. Many operations will be automated.

Roaming bands of hoodlums traveling in vans and panel trucks will terrorize suburban and rural communities, robbing, stealing, kidnapping and raping. Citizens will meet the violence with shotgun justice, forming vigilante groups in their frustration. There will be no confidence in the criminal justice system.

The pendulum will eventually swing the other way, and the government will crack down ruthlessly. Severe penalties will be established, out of proportion to some of the crimes to which they are applied. Civil liberties will be restricted, as police and investigative agencies are given broad powers of interrogation and arrest.

The crackdown on crime and violence will stop short of total gun control, and citizens without criminal records or histories of mental illness will still be permitted to own weapons. Laws regulating ownership and use of handguns will be more strictly enforced, however, and penalties will be strengthened for violations.

The office of President will be much stronger than it is today. He will be able to change laws he disagrees with simply by announcing his decisions in the news media. Eventually the President and other citizens will be able to stroll alone safely in the streets, but this will be long after the year 2000.

THE NEW WORLD

Communism will decline as a political philosophy and system of government after the year 2000, following one violent, last-ditch effort to achieve world dominance.

Japan, Canada and federations of the African and the West Indian nations will become the strong, affluent leaders of the new world. Mainland China will retain Communism but will gain the goodwill of the new powers, especially the African and West Indies federations, with political and material support during the years they are building their strength.

Portions of Central America will join the West Indian Federation. The federations will not have common governments, but instead will pool their material and political resources to compete better with other nations of the world.

The new federations will vault into technological prominence by accepting scientists emigrating from Russia, Eastern Europe and the United States so that they can work for peace instead of on weapons of war. The scientists will be attracted to the West Indies and Africa by generous government subsidies, freedom to work on projects of their choice and pleasant climates.

The decline of world Communism and of the United States, their powerful northern neighbor, will lead to stabilization of the previously shaky governments of South America. Free from outside agitation, the South American nations will build their economies and take their place as equal partners with other countries in the world.

The United Nations will survive to the year 2000 but will be so weakened by its ineffectiveness in crises that it will wither and die shortly thereafter. The world will have to seek other paths to peace.

Dr. Ernesto A. Montgomery
Universal Metaphysical Church
P.O. Box 19549
Los Angeles, Calif. 90019

Notes

INTRODUCTION

1. Many of Dr. Montgomery's predictions were carried in *Proud Minorities,* a weekly newspaper, now defunct, which served the black community in the Los Angeles area.

PART 1

CHAPTER 1

1. *Crusade in Europe* by Dwight D. Eisenhower (Doubleday, 1948).
2. *Breakthrough to Creativity: Your Higher Sense Perception* by Shafica Karagulla, M.D. (DeVorss, 1967).

CHAPTER 4

1. *The Spear of Destiny* by Trevor Ravenscroft (Putnam, 1973).
2. *Astrological Guide to the Presidential Candidates* by Sybil Leek (Abelard-Schuman, 1972).
3. *The Occult and the Third Reich* by Jean-Michel Angebert (Macmillan, 1974). Jean-Michel Angebert is the joint signature of two French scholars, Michel Bertrand and Jean Angelini.
4. *Zodiac and Swastika, How Astrology Guided Hitler's Germany,* by Wilhelm Wulff (Coward, McCann, 1973).
5. *The Occult Reich* by J. H. Brennan (New American Library, 1974).

CHAPTER 5

1. *The Astral Journey: Evidence for Out-of-Body Experiences from Socrates to the ESP Laboratory,* by Herbert B. Greenhouse (Doubleday, 1975).
2. *Journeys Out of the Body* by Robert A. Monroe (Doubleday, 1971).
3. *Probe The Unknown,* July 1975.

4. *ECKANKAR, the Key to Secret Worlds* by Paul Twitchell (Lancer Bks., 1969).

5. Author J. H. Brennan, in *The Occult Reich,* tells of a "Fräulein Anna Sprengler, who was a German adept and member of a secret order in Nuremberg. Fräulein Sprengler, Brennan says, helped the magicians of Victorian London formulate the rituals and established the doctrines of the Golden Dawn.

6. *The National Tattler,* March 2, 1975, Vol. 22, No. 9, page 28.

CHAPTER 6
1. *Psychic Discoveries Behind the Iron Curtain* by Sheila Ostrander and Lynn Schroeder (Prentice-Hall, 1970).
2. *Ibid.,* Chapter One, "A Riddle Wrapped in an Enigma."

PART 2

CHAPTER 2
1. *Winston Churchill* by Victor L. Albjerg (Twayne Publishers, 1973).
2. *Ibid.*
3. *Ibid.*

CHAPTER 3
1. From a copyrighted story by James Kerr in *The National Tattler,* Vol. 19, No. 21, November 25, 1973.
2. *Ibid.*

CHAPTER 4
1. *Marilyn: The Last Months,* by Eunice Murray with Rose Shade (Pyramid Books, 1975).

PART 3

CHAPTER 1
1. *UFOs: Interplanetary Visitors* by Raymond E. Fowler (Exposition Press, 1974). (Fowler is a regional investigator for the National Investigations Committee on Aerial Phenomena, NICAP, and has been studying UFOs for more than twenty-five years.)

Bibliography

Albjerg, Victor L. *Winston Churchill.* New York: Twayne Publishers, 1973.

Angebert, Jean-Michel. *The Occult and the Third Reich.* New York: Macmillan Publishing Co., 1974.

Bird, Lieutenant Colonel Eugene K. *Prisoner #7: Rudolf Hess.* New York: Viking Press, 1974.

Blair, Clay, Jr. *Silent Victory.* Philadelphia: J. B. Lippincott Co., 1975.

Blum, Ralph and Judy. *Beyond Earth: Man's Contact with UFOs.* New York: Bantam Books, 1974.

Blumenson, Martin. *The Patton Papers 1940–1945.* Boston: Houghton Mifflin Co., 1974.

Brennan, J. H. *The Occult Reich.* New York: Signet, New American Library, 1974.

Brissaud, Andre. *Canaris.* New York: Grossett & Dunlap, 1974.

Cavendish, Richard. *Encyclopedia of the Unexplained.* New York: McGraw-Hill Book Co., 1974.

Christopher, Milbourne. *Mediums, Mystics & the Occult.* New York: Thomas Y. Crowell Co., 1975.

Dubin, Reese P. *Telecult Power: The Amazing New Way to Psychic and Occult Wonders.* West Nyack, N.Y.: Parker Publishing Co., 1970.

Ebon, Martin. *The Riddle of the Bermuda Triangle.* New York: Signet, New American Library, 1975.

Eisenhower, Dwight D. *Crusade in Europe.* Garden City, N.Y.: Doubleday & Co., 1948.

Fest, Joachim C. *Hitler.* New York: Harcourt Brace Jovanovich, 1974.

Fowler, Raymond E. *UFOs: Interplanetary Visitors.* Jericho, N.Y.: Exposition Press, 1974.

Freedland, Nat. *The Occult Explosion.* New York: G. P. Putnam's Sons, 1972.

Frischauer, Willi. *Himmler the Evil Genius of the Third Reich.* New York: Belmont Books, 1953.

Geller, Uri. *Uri Geller: My Story.* New York: Praeger Publishers, 1975.

Glass, Justine. *They Foresaw the Future.* New York: G. P. Putnam's Sons, 1969.

Godwin, John. *Occult America.* Garden City, N.Y.: Doubleday & Co., 1972.

———. *Super Psychic.* New York: Pocket Books, 1974.

Greenhouse, Herbert B. *The Astral Journey.* Garden City, N.Y.: Doubleday & Co., 1975.

Hammond, David. *The Search for Psychic Power.* New York: Bantam Books, 1975.

Hammond, Sally. *We Are All Healers.* New York: Ballantine Books, 1973.

Karagulla, Dr. Shafica. *Breakthrough to Creativity.* Santa Monica, Calif.: DeVorss & Co., 1967.

MacNeice, Louis. *Astrology.* Garden City, N.Y.: Doubleday & Co., 1964.

Mishlove, Jeffrey. *The Roots of Consciousness.* New York: Random House, 1975.

Monroe, Robert A. *Journeys Out of the Body.* Garden City, N.Y.: Doubleday & Co., 1971.

Mosley, Leonard. *The Reich Marshal: A Biography of Hermann Goering.* Garden City, N.Y.: Doubleday & Co., 1974.

Murray, Eunice, with Shade, Rose. *Marilyn: The Last Months.* New York: Pyramid Books, 1975.

Nebel, Long John, with Teller, Sanford M. *The Psychic World Around Us.* New York: Hawthorn Books, 1969.

Ostrander, Sheila, and Schroeder, Lynn. *Psychic Discoveries Behind the Iron Curtain.* Englewood Cliffs, N.J.: Prentice-Hall, 1970.

Oyle, Dr. Irving. *The Healing Mind.* Millbrae, Calif.: Celestial Arts, 1975.

Ravenscroft, Trevor. *The Spear of Destiny.* New York: G. P. Putnam's Sons, 1973.

St. Clair, David. *How Your Psychic Powers Can Make You Rich.* New York: Bantam Books, 1975.

———. *Psychic Healers.* Garden City, N.Y.: Doubleday & Co., 1974.

Schiller, Lawrence, and Atkins, Susan. *The Killing of Sharon Tate.* New York: Signet, New American Library, 1969.

Shealy, Dr. C. Norman. *Occult Medicine Can Save Your Life.* New York: The Dial Press, 1975.

Steiger, Brad. *The Psychic Feats of Olof Jonsson.* Englewood Cliffs, N.J.: Prentice-Hall, 1971.

—— and Smith, Warren. *Satan's Assassins.* New York: Lancer Books, 1971.

Twitchell, Paul. *ECKANKAR.* New York: Lancer Books, 1969.

Uphoff, Walter and Mary Jo. *New Psychic Frontiers.* Gerrards Cross, Buckinghamshire, England: Colin Smythe, 1975.

Valentine, Tom. *Psychic Surgery.* Chicago: Henry Regnery Co., 1973.

Wiehl, Andrew. *Creative Visualization.* New York: Greenwich Book Publishers, 1958.

Wilson, Colin. *The Occult.* New York: Random House, 1971.

Wulff, Wilhelm. *Zodiac and Swastika.* New York: Coward, McCann & Geoghegan, 1973.